W9-CHI-965

Young Musicians
in World History

Young Musicians in World History

IRENE EARLS

GREENWOOD PRESS
Westport, Connecticut • London

Library of Congress Cataloging-in-Publication Data

Earls, Irene.
    Young musicians in world history / by Irene Earls.
      p. cm.
    Includes bibliographical references (p.) and index.
    Contents: Louis Armstrong—Johann Sebastian Bach—Ludwig van Beethoven—Pablo Casals—Sarah Chang—Ray Charles—Charlotte Church—Bob Dylan—John Lennon—Midori—Wolfgang Mozart—Niccolò Paganini—Isaac Stern.
    Summary: Profiles thirteen musicians who achieved high honors and fame before the age of twenty-five, representing many different time periods and musical styles.
    ISBN 0-313-31442-X (alk. paper)
      1. Musicians—Biography—Juvenile literature. [1. Musicians.]
    ML3929.E27 2002
    780'.92'2—dc21   2001040559
    [B]

British Library Cataloguing in Publication Data is available.

Library of Congress Catalog Card Number: 2001040559
ISBN: 0-313-31442-X

First published in 2002

Greenwood Press, 88 Post Road West, Westport, CT 06881
An imprint of Greenwood Publishing Group, Inc.
www.greenwood.com

Printed in the United States of America

The paper used in this book complies with the Permanent Paper Standard issued by the National Information Standards Organization (Z39.48–1984).

10 9 8 7 6 5 4 3 2 1

Contents

♪

Preface

This book brings together men and women who found success and world acclaim through musical gifts that were evident at an early age. Only two common traits exist among them: their genius for music and their ultimate success.

Their lives differed in myriad ways. Some lived a fortunate and happy childhood, born to the privileges of wealth or a comfortable home. Others were hungry and sick, born to poverty and deprivation. Some suffered indignation and humiliation. Some still create and perform even though time and success have changed their lives.

A wealth of young people have existed throughout history who could have been included in this volume. The thirteen who were ultimately selected to be profiled here were chosen with great care and consideration. The goal was to provide role models who came from different types of backgrounds and different periods in history. Many were selected because they had to rise above adversity in order to achieve. All became publicly successful before age twenty-five.

A number of sources were used to gather information on each individual. Some of these sources contradict each other. Different opinions and statistics, even different birth dates, surfaced; and inconsistencies in biographical data appeared. A major disadvantage arises when investigating the gifted: Written histories change with time. Authors exaggerate certain facts, alter, glamorize, minimize, and eliminate as they choose at the expense of what is correct. I have made every effort to check data and to provide reliable information. In *Young Musicians in World History*, the reader will find an unbiased view.

Entries are in alphabetical sequence by subject's last name. A brief bibliography follows each entry. A glossary of selected terms is included, although short definitions of some words are included within the text for the reader's ease.

Special thanks to Ed Earls, who helped with numerous details, and William Miller, University of Missouri, Edward DeZurko, University of Georgia, Edgar (Ned) Newland, University of New Mexico; and Fernand Beaucour, Centre d'Études Napoléoniennes, Paris. Also, special thanks to librarians Sandra Steele, Connie Maxey, Ann Black, Judy Schmidt, and Sue Vogt. Greenwood acquisitions editor Debby Adams is any author's dream; so is Danielle Bleam, her assistant.

♪

Introduction

In the history of the world, several centuries have produced musicians with talents so far beyond the ordinary that no measurement exists. Some had gifts too large and thus stumbled and fell, the gifts having never matured. Some had family support, lessons, and everything else needed to develop fully. Others had only talent and tenacity.

One might wonder how a three-year-old can play the violin with technical brilliance within a few months of touching the instrument for the first time and produce music with a degree of sensitivity and accomplishment that the majority of adults never achieve no matter how long they practice. In searching for an answer, one can only pinpoint the phenomenal achievers, men and women who walked a path no one else saw and listened to a beat no one else heard. Yet in examining individual lives, one finds no personality patterns, no substantial or subtle similarities in stature, no sameness of environment, no special personal relations, no idiosyncratic habits. Every one is different.

One's first inclination is to think that each child who produced beyond the expected human capacity had the best of everything life could provide. Indeed, a few prodigies experienced the unique world of privilege, ate the best food, and had expert training, medical care, tutors, and private education. Yet some prodigies endured poverty and racism. Some lost their parents at an early age. Some nearly starved. Some overcame personal obstacles that would have made the ordinary person collapse.

Collectively these prodigies were blind, orphaned, subjects of racist hate, privileged and beautiful, provided for and loved. All, regardless of personal circumstances, persevered and made it, and they made it big. How did they do it?

Young Musicians in World History provides information that may help answer this question. The book presents the lives and accomplishments of young women and men who pushed themselves beyond normal boundaries, sometimes against dreadful adversaries. Each individual worked with resoluteness and resolve to the total exclusion of all else. Not one let a single obstacle stand in the path of that star only he or she could see, or the voice only he or she could hear. Bob Dylan, who left home with nothing and headed alone for the dangers of life, believes anyone can achieve greatness: "We've all got it within us, for whatever we want to grasp for" (Shelton, p. 13). Yet some musicians found impediments to greatness and accomplishment. Even Dylan himself wrote about the force that struggled to stop him: "I ran from it when I was 10, 12, 13, 14, 15½, 17 an' 18. I been caught an' brought back all but once" (Shelton, p. 24).

Louis Armstrong, born into utter poverty, learned the trumpet in reform school: "one of the supervisors of the home, Mr. Peter Davis, . . . taught Louis to play the trumpet" (Panassié, p. 4). Armstrong ultimately became a player of precise, disciplined power and technical mastery, one of the greatest the world might ever see.

Johann Sebastian Bach, seventeenth-century organist and composer, played the violin practically in his cradle, as soon as his tiny hands could hold an instrument (a baby replica made especially for him). His gift to the world was some of the most complex music ears will ever hear. Yet Bach lived following one of the blackest periods in German history, 1618–1648, the time of the Thirty Years' War. This religious conflict reduced Germany to ruin and rubble from one end to the other. Mercenary armies massacred most of the peasant population with utter brutality and disregard for life. Moreover, what the vast mercenary armies did not burn, plunder, and destroy, disease did. This is what Bach knew: war ruins and sickness. But he did not pity himself; he did not blame anyone for his ruined country or the early deaths of his mother and father from disease. He chose not to waste his life feeling sorry or fighting what had passed. He chose instead to create. Today, some of his masterpieces cannot be played properly by many accomplished musicians, so complex are their intricacies. Jailed for a month, even in his cell he never rested. Instead, he composed a collection of choral preludes that form a dictionary of his language in sound.

Historians consider German composer Ludwig van Beethoven one of the most influential musicians in the history of music. Trained to the point of excess and abuse as a small child, Beethoven gave his first public performance at age eight. His mother died of tuberculosis and his father drank himself to death. Around age thirty he began not hearing notes from the piano and within twenty years was totally deaf. Despite numerous hardships Beethoven never stopped composing.

Many scholars consider Pablo Casals, late nineteenth-, early twentieth-century Spanish violoncellist, conductor, and composer, the world's greatest violoncellist. A child prodigy at age six, Casals played the piano and wrote and transposed music with the talent and maturity of an adult.

Sarah Chang, a twentieth-century Asian American violinist, began playing the violin when she was four years old. She had loving parents who helped keep her grounded, who never pushed her to practice. Today she plays brilliantly the most technically difficult compositions known in the history of music.

Ray Charles, a twentieth-century musical genius, suffered unimaginable miseries and adversities as a youth. He watched helplessly the death of his brother at age five. By the time he was six years old, he could not see. Born illegitimate, he endured his young mother's death when he was fourteen. An orphan with no family, blind, and living in the racist, segregated South in the 1940s, Charles had to leave everything he was familiar with and move to a segregated orphanage for blind children. Yet, throughout these hardships, sometimes virtually starving, he played the piano, sang and wrote stunning arrangements that changed twentieth-century music throughout not only the United States but the entire world.

Welsh soprano Charlotte Church, born with an extraordinary natural singing voice, first appeared on stage at the age of three and a half. By the time she reached her eighth birthday she drew crowds of every age who loved the purity and beauty of her voice. At the age of eleven, after singing over the phone for a television producer, she was invited to perform on television. She made a million-dollar, best-seller compact disc *Voice of an Angel* at age thirteen. Church won a place in *The Guinness Book of Records* as the youngest solo artist ever to achieve a top-thirty album on the U.S. charts.

Bob Dylan, twentieth-century American singer and songwriter, became a uniquely accomplished guitarist by age ten and seemed destined to spend his life precariously on the move—as he says, "[with] one foot on the highway, and one foot in the grave" (Shelton, p. 429). In his teens he composed controversial, completely original songs, all unequaled, all unrivaled. His songs express the cultural and political scene of the 1960s and thereafter. Born in 1941, Dylan has been a distinctive, influential voice of American popular culture. He has composed over two hundred exceptional songs, many interpreted by other performers. His work remains unmatched.

John Lennon, British singer, musician, songwriter, and author, organized the Beatles while in his teens. The Beatles became a twentieth-century phenomenon, a delightful and occasionally cacophonous uproar that soared beyond social classes, age groups, intellectual levels, and even geographic areas. Lennon wrote most of the songs performed by the group. Contrary to what most people think, he never had an easy life. "He had a wayward and absentee father, a frivolous mother who died at a critical point in his life, a domineering aunt, and two wives of utterly contrasting personalities" (Coleman, p. 41).

Even the harshest critics cite Midori, spectacular Japanese-born prodigy, as the most distinguished violinist of the latter part of the twentieth century. Although she played a Paganini *Caprice* before an audience at age six, her real public career began at age ten. She received a standing ovation after an impressive debut with the New York Philharmonic at age eleven, and before she reached her teens she played at the White House. By the time she was fourteen the best audiences throughout the world recognized her name.

Wolfgang Amadeus Mozart, eighteenth-century composer born in Salzburg, Austria, is, according to many historians, the foremost child prodigy of the music world. He represents one of the highest peaks in the history of music: "for many people Mozart is the greatest of composers. No words can do justice to his simplicity or his sublimity; he is, like Shakespeare, ageless" (Baker, p. 9). At age six his father presented him and his older sister, Maria Anna (Nannerl), in concerts at the court of Empress Maria Theresa in Vienna. He also introduced them to the principal aristocratic households of central Europe, London, and Paris. In later years, while his father lay ill and close to death, Mozart and his sister could not touch the piano. To keep himself busy, the child composed his first symphony for every single instrument of the orchestra. He was eight years old. By age thirteen he had composed concertos, sonatas, symphonies, a German operetta, and an Italian opera buffa (comedy).

Born into poverty, violinist Niccolò Paganini performed with such force and passion that those who heard him claimed he had the devil guiding his bow. From the time he could hold an instrument he practiced to the point of collapse from morning until night seven days a week under the stern eye of his father who withheld food as punishment. So beautiful was his music that many who heard him play spoke of him as a figure from heaven. Nothing deterred him; he nearly died from measles and became deathly sick with scarlet fever. Diligence, persistence and hours of hard work made Paganini a virtuoso who became a legend.

The world acknowledges Isaac Stern, twentieth-century Russian-born violinist, as the first American violin virtuoso. His gift appeared early when he learned the piano at age six and the violin at age eight. By the time he reached his eleventh birthday, he had made his debut. He never stopped. All his life he was a greatly loved performing artist, famous for his extraordinary music, his love of life, his unfaltering dedication to sharing his knowledge with younger musicians, and his kind and generous personality. As one of the most revered musicians in the world, he was a crucial figure and spokesperson in music. Still persevering and indomitable, he published a book with the writer Chaim Potok in 1999, *Isaac Stern, My First 79 Years*.

In brief, the individuals represented here gave their earliest years and their entire lives to music. Despite unimaginable obstacles and setbacks they forged on, driven, reaching out, climbing higher and higher. Some remain tenacious and relentless far into their careers.

Many prodigies came from musical families. Mozart had a brilliant sister, a musician. Midori's mother and Sarah Chang's father are violinists. Johann Sebastian Bach came from a family of musicians, poor in material possessions but wealthy in love and music. A few prodigies were educated and guided carefully. Others, such as Ray Charles and Louis Armstrong, had no musical inheritance, no one to care for them, and no money to buy an instrument; they persevered alone.

A few geniuses have been the subjects of exaggerated legend. A few chose to become hermits. Some avoided people and hid from a world they knew could be cruel. Some, like Beethoven, never married. Some suffered physical handicaps. Ray Charles is blind. Beethoven became stone-deaf and very ill, yet he persevered and rose to heights even he had never attained previously.

The individuals described here displayed enormous energy and productivity and inspiration. They suffered, they created, they charted their lives through a sometimes dark tunnel with a gift, a talent they could neither deny nor hide. They offered no commercials to their audiences, only personal accomplishments.

The musicians discussed here aimed for something far beyond the everyday in their lives. On the long roads they traveled, they touched life's most ecstatic and most dreadful edges. They found inspiration for music everywhere they looked. Not one let the largest obstacle become a deterrent.

Bibliography

Baker, Richard. *Mozart*. New York: Thames and Hudson, 1982.

Coleman, Ray. *Lennon: The Definitive Biography*. New York: Harper-Perennial, 1992.

Panassié, Hugues. *Louis Armstrong*. New York: Charles Scribner's Sons, 1971.

Shelton, Robert. *No Direction Home*. New York: Da Capo Press, 1997.

Young Musicians
in World History

♪

Louis Armstrong

(1898/1900?–1971)

Daniel Louis Armstrong (also known as Satchmo and Satchelmouth), New Orleans trumpeter, singer, and band leader, changed almost singlehandedly the American concept of jazz. He invented an extraordinary type of fast fingering on the trumpet no one could copy, and he improvised music with a style no one could imitate. He decorated melody, filling it out in an extreme way that produced original, complicated solos. He also composed while on stage in performance. And he did all this without ever having had a music lesson. The trumpet is an instrument for which one needs training to play correctly, and Armstrong played so incorrectly that he ruined his lip permanently. He had no musical instrument of his own until he was seventeen years old. Having never been trained, he was an adult before he learned to read music.

With unique trumpet solos and a powerful voice, Armstrong led American jazz away from the narrow structure in which it had existed for decades. After hearing his work, more than one musician felt inspired to "jazz up" his own music. Armstrong's career spanned more than fifty-five years, and as "the Einstein of jazz he is generally credited with the role of primary shaper of the art" (Scholes, p. 52).

Born in New Orleans, Louisiana, sometime in 1898 or 1900, Armstrong was the first great jazz soloist to make gramophone records. From the time he learned the trumpet in reform school at around age twelve, he became the finest trumpeter New Orleans has ever known. Also, historians think Armstrong contributed more than any other musician to what jazz became in Chicago in the middle

1920s. They claim that his gift was so remarkable it influenced not only jazz but eventually nearly the whole field of Western popular music.

Louis Armstrong

It would be impossible to overestimate Armstrong's importance to twentieth-century music, and yet, always a humble man, he never regarded his career as a move toward stardom, the stage, money, or any kind of importance to music or history. In some ways his life changed little after he became a world-famous star.

As a youth, Armstrong never saw a day without poverty and the restrictions of segregation. He was never free to wander around his own city outside the black ghetto, a place so rough residents called it the Battlefield. He could not go to movies or shows or restaurants (except ones for blacks only). He could not enter a white family's house through the front door. He had to take off his hat to white children his own age and, with respect, do what they told him to do. Even after he found world fame, his life and the life of the musicians with whom he worked remained the same.

> [Being] a star turned out to be not quite so wonderful as it sounded. . . . The musicians, being blacks, could not eat at most restaurants, nor sleep in most hotels, nor even use the rest rooms at ordinary gas stations. They traveled on old, bumpy buses, they slept in rooms rented in private homes in black neighborhoods. When they couldn't find a black restaurant, the manager or some other white would have to go into a store and order sandwiches for them all, which they would eat on the bus. (Collier, 1985, p. 119)

Despite the extreme limitations his black heritage and poverty brought him, at a young age the determined and gifted Armstrong became a major player on the world stage of music. Eventually millions recognized him as the symbol of jazz.

Before Armstrong, the collective identity of the ensemble had always been primary in jazz music, but Armstrong made the trumpet soloist distinguished because of his own unbelievable virtuosity. Not only did he go far beyond other players on the trumpet, but his unique singing completely dismantled traditional ideas concerning popular music. Jazz singing hardly existed outside the blues field in the first two decades of the twentieth century. So distinctive were Armstrong's voice and trumpet that many times when he performed, his voice and horn so powerful, other musicians made him stand away from the band.

Armstrong's life in music began at a young age. Although individual references speak with authority concerning dates and events, the actual details of his childhood are inconsistent. Even his full name is in doubt: One sees both Daniel Louis and Louis Daniel. Historians may never verify the name of the street where he was born in New Orleans. They also argue the age at which he learned to play the cornet (a brass-wind musical instrument of the trumpet class having three valves). He spent time in reform school, but the date of his entry there is uncertain. Even the fact that he learned to play the trumpet in reform school is in disagreement.

Armstrong himself claimed he was born in New Orleans in James Alley (or Jane Alley). The alley was a small and overcrowded lane about a block long in what city people called the "back o' town" district. All accounts paint the area as dark, dirty, and dangerous. As a child, Louis wore dresses because there was nothing else for him to wear. He witnessed knife fights. Most agree he saw in James Alley the lowest types of bums, drunks, robbers, and women walking the streets at night. Later, so rotted and rat-infested were the buildings bordering the alley that the city of New Orleans demolished each one as the black inhabitants died or moved away.

The majority of accounts agree that Louis Armstrong was born in a one-room, backyard wooden building approached by a narrow alleyway from James Alley. The building measured about twenty-six by twenty-four feet and had one room divided by upright boards into two or three sections. It had no running water and no facilities. Rainwater collected outside in a tub. After Armstrong became famous and the wooden structure was purchased for preservation, preservationists described the building as unfit for human habitation.

Armstrong's birth date is most often given as July 4, 1900. No birth certificates exist for either his parents or him. No records exist from the three years he spent at Fisk elementary school. Only his life as a child gives historians one arena in which to agree: The boy had a rough childhood that would have kept most boys on the street, never to be educated, never to leave the alley, always to be beaten down and poor, probably to live as a thief or in a jail cell.

Armstrong never had a family life. He claims he did not see his sister until he was five years old. He played in the dirt with twigs and junk. Because he did not know when he was born, he never had a birthday party. He lived on beans and rice, with occasional scraps of fish. After learning little, he left his segregated slum school (which had few books and no cafeteria) after the third grade. When his parents split up, he didn't see his father, Willie, until he was grown. Willie worked most of his life in a turpentine factory near James Alley. He died when Armstrong was thirty-three years old. Mayann (Mary Ann), his mother, lived as a servant to a white family in New Orleans. She had married Willie at age fifteen. Young, seeking happiness, sometimes she disappeared for days and forgot about Louis.

No historian has been able to explain Armstrong's musical inheritance. No one can explain his natural ability for the trumpet. Some seed of precocious artistic genius lurked within him from birth, a fortunate gift because young Louis Armstrong had nothing else. He had no benefits and no comforts. His parents could barely read and write. There was seldom money for food, much less for clothes or shoes, and the thought of owning a musical instrument was absurd.

More often than not, Armstrong had neither mother nor father to love and feed him, so he lived with his grandmother or on the streets or in a reformatory. He survived severe emotional upsets, hunger, sickness with no care, bare feet even in winter. In later years he believed that his childhood struggles gave him the strength he possessed as an adult and the determination to succeed. Also, he developed a strong belief in education because of his deprived childhood. He wrote in 1970 that he never saw his father write at all. In fact, he didn't see Willie do anything that would set an example, and he knew his mother could barely read and write.

Before he reached his teens, playing games or dancing and singing in the streets, Armstrong began to absorb New Orleans Negro folk tunes and religious music. Churches and different religions and even voodoo surrounded him, with the various ways to worship always attracting a large, loud, and sincere following. From the time he could barely walk, Louis's grandmother took him to church where he learned his singing methods by listening.

Despite adversity, Armstrong grew up honest, good, and kind. His mother, Mayann, may have been nearly illiterate, but she taught him not to fight, never to steal, and always to treat others with respect.

Because he genuinely loved her, he listened to what she told him. In his harsh surroundings, however, he could barely live up to her admonishments. In fact, the company surrounding him got rougher as he grew older. When he left his grandmother to live with Mayann, he moved into an even more depressed neighborhood. He frequented saloons with pianists and dance halls with ear-splitting ragtime bands.

Armstrong picked up jazz following New Orleans street parades, listening to funeral music or singing on the dockside with friends from his local gang. Their music became distinct, and knowledgeable musicians called it ragtime. Whenever there was a dance or a lawn party, Louis's band of six of his closest friends would stand within hearing distance and play ragtime. Small ragtime bands were usually made up of cornet or trumpet, clarinet, trombone, and a rhythm section that included bass, drums, and guitar. At the same time, jazz was beginning to form, and Louis fell in love with it.

In New Orleans music was everywhere. Louis heard it when he went to sleep at night and when he awoke in the morning (some places stayed open day and night). He heard it while he was in school as bands walked past outside. Funeral bands marched the streets slowly, and advertisement bands rode by in wagons. Bands played at picnics, baseball games, and horse races and in parks. With no television to watch and no books to read, music was listened to everywhere.

Without music, Armstrong would have had no future. Even as young as age seven, he had taken odd jobs to help his mother buy food. He had no interest in the turpentine factory where, later, his half-brother worked. He sold newspapers on St. Charles Street, and a year or two later he worked at the Konowski family's coal business, filling buckets on a wagon to sell at five cents a bucket. Always with music on his mind, he formed a quartet. He and the boys went out after supper and sang along Rampart Street and made extra money.

♪
Louis Armstrong

Born:
Exact date unknown:
July 4, 1900?
New Orleans, Louisiana
Died:
July 6, 1971
Corona, New York
Date of First Recording:
April 5, 1923

At age twelve Armstrong, who ran loose and fought in the streets with other boys, was arrested. One New Orleans musician suggested the authorities had been watching him for a few months because of Mayann's undesirable influences. He said his mother never discussed her line of work and never allowed him to see her activities, but he knew how she made money besides washing clothes and working as a servant. The city considered her unfit as a parent and decided he would have better care in the Colored Waifs' Home.

One evening, New Year's Eve 1912 or 1913, as the quartet sang, a boy fired a cap pistol near Louis's face. Louis carried a real gun (some accounts say he used blanks), and when friends encouraged him to go after the boy, he did. Then the police arrested him. A judge sentenced him to serve an indefinite term at the Colored Waifs' Home (reform school) for discharging firearms within the city limits. According to one account, he was twelve years old at the time. Another account says he was thirteen. Armstrong has written it was New Year's Day (Collier, 1985, p. 25).

The Colored Waifs' Home, or reformatory became a turning point in Armstrong's life. For the first time he had food every day, clean clothes, shoes, and people who cared about what he did. Some historians believe that while he was in the home he learned to play the trumpet beyond anything amateur. (Others say he already played well enough to entertain.) Two musicians taught him in the reformatory. Some historians disagree with this detail. They believe he played too well, having picked up what he knew on the street. Some say he had played the trumpet a little before entering the reform school, an establishment run like a military camp, and he played it there every day. "It was he [Louis] who now blew calls in the home for waking up, for soup, for baths" (Panassié, p. 5).

At the end of his stay in the reformatory, Louis, fourteen years old, knew how to play marches and many different, even sophisticated songs. Most important, he had developed his own style, his own method of fingering. For the next few years he worked at different day jobs selling newspapers, delivering milk, collecting for a scrap merchant, selling coal, and unloading banana boats. After he left the reform school, he only occasionally performed musically and hardly touched a trumpet for two years. Then he began filling in for musicians who called in sick at the last minute or didn't show up for work. Whenever a musician would stay home, someone would suggest they find little Louis.

Armstrong claims he went every time they called because he was crazy about the music and loved to play his horn fast. In fact, he played it so fast he left other players behind. They told him to cut down on the fast fingering (which he did naturally) or find somewhere else to play.

Nothing Armstrong did in the early days of his youth explains his prodigious ability at fast fingering except the talent with which he was born. With no training, he could play anything he could whistle or anything he heard, and he drew crowds everywhere he played. Armstrong worked with other players between the years 1910 and 1917, or from the time he was ten years old until he was seventeen. When he began playing steadily, his technique improved and advanced rapidly. Still, he worked in places where shootings and police raids were not unusual. Even in 1918, Armstrong, then age eighteen, had to keep his job selling coal because jobs with musicians were not steady. A war was on (World War I), and the slogan was "work or fight." He stopped selling coal on Armistice Day, 1918. After the war he married Daisy Parker, a twenty-one-year-old prostitute. Daisy could neither read nor write. Armstrong always said even if she was illiterate, she knew how to fuss and fight. Many times, both of them went to jail for fighting in the streets. (He divorced Daisy in 1923 in order to marry Lillian Hardin.) Living into her fifties, Daisy took pride in knowing Louis and never acknowledged their divorce.

During this time, Armstrong played on excursions out of New Orleans on the Mississippi riverboats. Playing long hours on the boat journeys proved to be a valuable experience, and his playing and music-reading improved.

When Armstrong was twenty-two years old, after playing funerals and serving an apprenticeship as a trumpeter in New Orleans cabarets and playing on the Mississippi riverboats, he was called to Chicago by Joe Oliver, a famous New Orleans–trained musician, to play second cornet in the orchestra of Joe "King" Oliver. Armstrong had been offered jobs away from home before, but he had always been doubtful of his readiness. After "Papa Joe" asked him to come to Lincoln Gardens in Chicago, Armstrong felt that nothing could hold him back.

In Chicago, at first Armstrong felt homesick and lost. The Creole jazz band sounded far better than he had anticipated, and in the beginning he felt intimidated. In fact, he wondered if he would be able to keep up with such formidable talent. After all, the trumpet is the hardest instrument to play, and Armstrong had had no formal training. Joe Oliver warned him, "You'll never get the trumpet, she'll get you" (Panassié, p. 47). The records reveal Armstrong had only one problem: His strong, one-of-a-kind voice frequently broke through the highly disciplined music. Also, because he could make his instrument sing as no other person in the band could, personal jealousies developed.

Armstrong's power of delivery and his new style added a chapter to the history of music. He was only twenty-two years old. Although he felt lonely, as he worked it didn't take long for his talent to push his inferior feelings aside. He surpassed everyone. On his first night in Chicago he listened, then rehearsed the next afternoon with the orchestra and after that quickly gained recognition. The rapport

> ♪
> **Interesting Facts about Louis Armstrong**
>
> He played the trumpet so incorrectly that he ruined his lip permanently.
>
> His voice and horn were so powerful that other musicians made him stand away from the band.
>
> He appeared in thirty-six movies.

achieved by Joe Oliver and Armstrong, the two-cornet breaks and leads and occasional solos, became overnight conversation among lovers of the new music. They especially loved Armstrong's solos.

Anyone born with Armstrong's gift and musical abilities would attract individuals who would try to direct him professionally. Armstrong, however, looked up to Joe Oliver as a sort of father-substitute, and "Papa Joe" directed him well during his teenage years and early twenties. In the end, however, Armstrong helped others far more than others had helped him. "[I]t [was] really Louis Armstrong who electrified and put on their own two feet, just about all the great jazzmen" (Panassié, p. 56). He influenced the style of orchestras and big bands and other musicians besides those who played trumpet—namely, guitar, piano, tenor saxophone, and trombone.

Mayann, Armstrong's mother, visited him in Chicago at Lincoln Gardens. Armstrong said he could barely believe his eyes when she walked through the door and saw him on the stage. Someone had told her he was a failure, and, not believing this, she went to Chicago to see for herself. Armstrong was so thrilled to see his mother that he rented her an apartment and bought her a new wardrobe. Not long after that she went back to New Orleans, and a little later she got sick and never recuperated. Mayann died in her early forties.

While in Chicago, Armstrong met Lillian Hardin. An intelligent musician, she had studied music at Fisk University, where she was class valedictorian. Originally from Memphis, Tennessee, she discovered she loved jazz after moving with her family to Chicago in 1917 and working with Delta jazzmen at the Dreamland Café, a typical cabaret or nightclub. Upon meeting Armstrong, she was surprised to see that "little Louis" weighed 226 pounds. According to Lillian, her disappointment in everything about him in the beginning was enormous. She didn't like his clothes or the way he talked. Later, though, "she began to realize that beneath the second hand suits and the atrocious ties was a shy, soft-spoken young man who always tried to be polite and courteous and never cause trouble for other people" (Collier, 1985, p. 71). She wondered why everyone called Armstrong "Li'l Louis," when he was so big. She was told friends gave him the nickname as he started following them around when he was a little boy. She didn't see him again until she moved to Joe Oliver's band at the Lincoln Gardens. Then, Joe Oliver told her that Louis was a better trumpet player than he'd ever be but he'd never let Louis get ahead, he'd always keep him playing second. After that the situation changed. When Lillian began going to recording sessions, she began paying more attention to Armstrong. Oliver and Armstrong were next to each other, and no one could hear any of Oliver's notes.

Armstrong's trumpet so overwhelmed the band and outplayed every musician that Oliver put him in a corner about fifteen feet away.

Lillian knew that if they had to move Louis that far away, he must be the better player. He had started to use a difficult technique known as rubato (modifying notes). Because he performed rubato naturally and perfectly, other musicians disliked him.

The band went on to record titles for Gennett, Okeh, Columbia, and Paramount, all during 1923, at which time Armstrong was twenty-three years old. He arrived in the recording studios as a gifted, accomplished musician. Some fellow musicians believe that while recording he probably held his performance back. Nevertheless, musicians today applaud his unusual tone, technical virtuosity, and remarkable ability even as it was inadequately captured by the yet-undeveloped recording technology of the 1920s. (The earliest gramophone records of jazz appeared around 1916, more than thirty years after Thomas A. Edison invented the phonograph in 1877.)

With a busy schedule traveling, recording, and performing, Armstrong still had an active personal life. He married Lillian Hardin on February 5, 1924. (They separated in 1931 and divorced in 1938. The same year, he married Alpha Smith in Houston, Texas.) It is interesting to note that the women in his life never changed his drive to move ahead, to keep perfecting what he already knew.

Armstrong's performances improved to the point that big names such as Fletcher Henderson and Erskine Tate featured him as an orchestra soloist. He became so successful as a soloist that by the end of the 1920s he had formed his own group of five musicians, the Louis Armstrong Hot Six. The group stopped playing a few weeks later, but then Armstrong expanded it and renamed the new group the Louis Armstrong Hot Seven. At this time, during the 1920s, Armstrong, just out of his teens, recorded a series of innovative performances that influenced jazz musicians not only in the United States but throughout the world of mass entertainment.

Jazz also appeared in the concert hall at this time, although it was usually billed under a sophisticated and euphemistic description such as "symphonized syncopation." Even some operas were rewritten and "jazzed up." Also, jazz spawned a dance mania that was probably more widespread than the craze for the waltz and the polka in the nineteenth century. Armstrong influenced the "jazz craze" that replaced the era of ragtime in the 1920s. Ragtime, usually played on a piano, consisted of regular melody lines, simply syncopated (with the use of shifting accents) over a four-square march-style bass.

By 1930 the world wanted jazz, and Armstrong stayed so busy he had no time for vacation. Beginning in 1932 with a crowning appearance in

England, he traveled to most countries of the world and became the foremost ambassador of American jazz music. Most people who listened to jazz in the early twentieth century believed the music was entirely new and unknown. Jazz, however, was not new. Historians trace the roots of jazz to American colonial days, the ultimate source, via the Caribbean islands, being the native music of Negro slaves.

Armstrong's natural talent continued to soar so high above that of other musicians who played with him that not one could touch the extraordinary, effortless quality of his music. Unfortunately, he made them appear mediocre. But Armstrong, even though he tried many times, could not hide his technical virtuosity. His personal record of performing, playing, singing, and practicing continued to improve; unlike other musicians, at no time did he find himself in a backslide. Whereas other musicians seemed to level off and find a plateau, Armstrong never followed this pattern. Regardless of sorrow or emotional upset, he inched forward with every hour of hard work.

The rudiments of his music evolved a persistent use of blues that fit color categories into which most music can be categorized. For example, some scholars describe Mozart's music as blue, Chopin's as green, Wagner's as luminous with changing colors. Beethoven has aroused the sensation of black. Rimsky-Korsakov has been associated with brownish-gold and bright yellow and sunny blue, sapphire, sparkling, somber, dark blue shot with steel (Scholes, pp. 202–204). Unbelievably, Armstrong is all of these. Add to his unheard-of coloration the disciplined power and technical mastery he perfected, and one finds a clarity of tone heard neither before nor since. Along with color is Armstrong's rhythmic resiliency rooted in an inimitable pulsating swing.

Of course Armstrong became famous. Once the world heard his music, he found no rest. Coast-to-coast tours in the United States began in 1940. In 1942, touring and practice took all his time. He divorced Alpha Smith (married since 1931) and married his fourth wife, Lucille Wilson, a woman more tolerant of his music's demands. Their marriage lasted until he died.

By the mid-1940s, a new big band was formed to accompany Armstrong. He starred at Esquire's Metropolitan Opera House concert in January 1944. During these and hundreds of other performances, Armstrong never changed his style for the more complex rhythmic and harmonic elements of the modern jazz that became popular in the 1940s. Instead, he brought to exquisite perfection the sparkling, classic, easily assimilated melodic improvising that he had so successfully developed during his childhood. An expert in the more introspective subtleties and nuances of the blues, he evolved to become an effusive, rhapsodic player of deeply felt feelings. A font of invention every time he played, Armstrong treated his listeners' ears to rhythms previously unheard.

Yet, even while changing completely the world of music, Armstrong's life never became easy. It seemed the highest hurdles such as the following met him at every turn:

> In 1960 M-G-M recorded Louis with Bing Crosby...this LP [long playing record] called *Bing and Satchmo* has Louis playing and singing with Bing Crosby and the Billy May Orchestra, sometimes with the addition of a choir. The orchestral background by Billy May was recorded *first*. This recording was then sent to Bing Crosby, who sang his part using earphones, which the M-G-M engineers mixed with the orchestral part. After that, it was all sent to Louis Armstrong and it was then his turn, also using earphones, to add his vocal and trumpet parts to the music already recorded. This procedure of recording the accompaniment first is a musical barbarism and especially harmful to music like jazz. (Panassié, p. 141)

No one knew how recordings were made, and everyone everywhere wanted to hear Louis Armstrong play and sing, though they never seemed to get the best of what he had to offer. He toured the world: Australia, East Asia, London, Africa, New Zealand, Mexico, Iceland, India, Singapore, Korea, Hawaii, Japan, Hong Kong, Formosa, East and West Germany, Czechoslovakia, Romania, Yugoslavia, Hungary, France, Holland, Scandinavia, and Great Britain, to name a few. He also appeared on numerous TV shows.

A few of the thirty-six movies in which Armstrong appeared are: *Pennies from Heaven, Goin' Places, A Song Is Born, Here Comes the Groom, The Glenn Miller Story, Satchmo the Great, The Beat Generation, Paris Blues, Disneyland after Dark, Where the Boys Meet the Girls,* and *Hello Dolly.* Producers filmed his movies all over the world.

The year he died, 1971, he played and sang on the *David Frost Show* with Bing Crosby. In March, Armstrong and the All Stars played a two-week engagement at the Empire Room of the Waldorf Astoria in New York. Soon after concluding this engagement, he entered the Beth Israel Hospital on March 15, having a heart attack. He remained in the intensive care unit until mid-April but left the hospital on May 6. On July 6 at 5:30 A.M. he died in his sleep at his home in Corona, New York.

Louis Armstrong was one of the most beloved entertainers in the world. A special message of sorrow came from the White House when President Richard Nixon expressed his condolences. Frank Sinatra, Bing Crosby, the governor of New York, the mayor of New York City, and fifteen thousand people appeared to hear jazz bands play at a special memorial service for him in New Orleans.

Louis Armstrong rose from poverty in a segregated social system designed to keep blacks in their place, and the result was that even as a world-famous star he never could go against the laws he had abided by all his life. Yet despite a lack of musical training, no family support, no education, and denial at restaurants and hotels, his genius and hard work took him to the top of the world of entertainment.

Bibliography

Collier, James Lincoln. *Louis Armstrong, an American Genius*. New York: Oxford University Press, 1983.

————. *Louis Armstrong, an American Success Story*. New York: Macmillan, 1985.

Jones, Max, and John Louis Chilton. *The Louis Armstrong Story 1900–1971*. New York: Da Capo Press, 1988.

Panassié, Hugues. *Louis Armstrong*. New York: Charles Scribner's Sons, 1971.

Scholes, Percy A. *The Oxford Companion to Music*, 10th ed. London: Oxford University Press, 1978.

♪

Johann Sebastian Bach

(1685–1750)

Historians consider Bach, a German musician, principally an organist and composer, the preeminent genius of seventeenth-century baroque music. One of the greatest forces in the history of music, Bach played the violin, clavichord, harpsichord, and organ. His compositions took polyphonic or "many sound" "many voice" baroque music to its height. Each part of one of his compositions moved in complex independence and freedom, though harmonically melding together. He composed masterful and vigorous works in almost every musical form of the seventeenth century. His phenomenal abilities with sound were evident when he was a child barely able to stand and hold a tiny violin.

During his career, he wrote hundreds of compositions that include close to three hundred religious and secular choral works known as cantatas (musical compositions consisting of vocal solos and choruses used as a setting for a story to be sung but not acted). His masterworks and arrangements stretched musical techniques such as counterpoint and fugue to extremes, to their most complex heights. In counterpoint, on a keyboard, the right hand plays one melody and the left hand plays a different melody. Both hands are played together to form a result so complex that some compositions exist that few musicians in the world have ever conquered correctly. Fugue is a composition in which different instruments repeat the main melody with extremely involved, inordinately difficult techniques that require a level of accomplishment and skill only the most gifted musicians are able to attain. Bach reveled in these compositions. He composed and played them with ease.

Johann Sebastian Bach was born at Eisenach, in Thuringia, Germany, on March 21, 1685. Even as a small child before he went to school, he indulged in the long and frequent music sessions enjoyed by his family. Family became and remained a large part of his life; even as a baby in his crib, he listened to family members make music. He loved to hear his relatives play and sing together and tell stories about his German ancestors, the accomplished, well-known Bachs.

Most of the Bachs lived in the German towns of Eisenach, Arnstadt, and Erfurt. Over the years, the name Bach became synonymous with

Johann Sebastian Bach

musician. Nearly everyone in the family wrote songs or created compositions and played them by ear for long, enjoyable hours of family entertainment. Written, played, and sung for pleasure, some were comical, some even loud, off-color, and bawdy. Musicians since they were children, family members could harmonize perfectly while at the same time taking tangents to unknown territory, creating their own fill-in songs as they played. In fact, the Bachs arranged so many extemporized songs that they named them *quodlibet*, Latin for "what you please." "In the Bach family, a *quodlibet* was an improvised song with humorous lyrics and, occasionally, with double meanings" (Reingold, p. 4).

It didn't occur to anyone that baby Johann Sebastian would not become a musician just like everyone else. It was only natural that as soon as his little hands could hold an instrument, his father gave him his first lessons on a tiny violin made especially for him. He learned to play it so rapidly and thoroughly and became so accomplished in other tasks relating to his education that by his eighth birthday he entered the gymnasium (the equivalent to high school).

During the seventeenth century, German school days were far different from American school days of today. Long and demanding of extreme discipline, they began early and ended late. Johann Sebastian attended fifteen hours of class (at age eight) from 6:00 in the morning until 9:00 at night in the summer, and from 7:00 until 10:00 in the dark and freezing German winter. Wednesdays and Saturdays were half-holidays because dismissal came early, at 3:00. On Sundays the child, who had an exceptional voice, sang in the St. George Church choir.

Bach spent long days in school, with music everywhere he turned, and with a settled and secure, loving family life (his parents and seven brothers and sisters) waiting for him every evening ready for more music. All of them participated in some sort of musical endeavor. His parents were not wealthy, but they lived an honest and happy life within modest means in a comfortable old house. They used the largest room strictly for music. This room, one the Bachs considered the most important in the house, had been expanded and expanded again until music consumed the entire first floor. Here, by the hour, Johann Sebastian listened to his father and his father's fellow musicians play their instruments. He listened to all kinds of music, even his older brothers practicing the oboe, trumpet, clavichord, and harpsichord (a keyboard instrument).

The fact that music could be such an important part of any family in the seventeenth century was a miracle. Bach's birth followed the Thirty Years' War, one of the most ruinous conflicts in the history of the world. Germans knew the horrors of merciless mercenary armies that fought from one end of the country to the other, and they rampaged for thirty years. This destructive war stunted German life and growth for more than one hundred years following the 1648 Treaty of Westphalia that finally ended the struggle. The German people remembered the incredible sufferings of their families for centuries thereafter, and the restoration and replacement of buildings and animals and land spanned generations.

One of the worst-devastated areas was Bach's birthplace, Thuringia. Here, half the families had been slaughtered or starved to death after huge armies plundered and raped and laid waste to everything in sight. They killed the horses and cattle and destroyed hundreds of thousands of acres of farmland. The spoiled land did not recover during Bach's lifetime.

During this time many literary figures, painters, sculptors, and other geniuses died from starvation and disease or fell victim to robbers or murderers. Fortunately, Bach survived, one of the few exceptions to the immeasurable loss in human creative talent and genius.

Bach was the youngest of the eight children of Johann Ambrosius Bach and his wife, Maria Elisabeth Lammerhirt. Director of town music, Bach's father had also served as leader of the town band in Arnstadt and as a violinist in Erfurt. Johann Sebastian first attended the Eisenach Latin School. His mother died unexpectedly in 1694. At the time, Bach had been in school for just one year and was only nine years old. Less than a year later, his father died. Indeed, death at an early age was a common event after the war. With the soil spoiled and rotting, bacteria ran rampant. There was no knowledge of sanitation. Fresh fruits and vegetables did not exist.

Johann Sebastian always remembered his father. Ambrosius Bach lived for only nine years after his son's birth and did not have time to start his son's instruction on the harpsichord, as he surely would have, had he survived. Johann Sebastian always remembered the early lessons on the tiny violin given by his father. Because of this, it became one of the instruments he preferred throughout most of his life.

After the death of both his parents, Johann Sebastian, orphaned a month before his tenth birthday, and his brother went to live with their oldest brother, who was an organist in the town of Ohrdruf. Here, in addition to demanding schoolwork, Johann Sebastian spent hours learning to play the organ, the harpsichord, and the clavichord (a stringed keyboard instrument). Even for a Bach, the child's progress amazed everyone. Johann Christoph, the brother who became his teacher, tried unsuccessfully to hold back his younger brother's rapid progress. Although this method of teaching cannot be explained, some scholars believe this was because he wanted the boy to learn slowly and thoroughly.

Johann Sebastian, however, could not be held back. His brother possessed a book of clavier pieces by the most famous masters of the day. (A clavier is any stringed instrument that has a keyboard—the piano, for example.) He begged his brother to allow him to study from the book, but his brother kept it locked away when not using it. After all, a book in the seventeenth century was a rare and expensive possession. Music manuscripts in the seventeenth century were few, precious, and beyond all but a few pocketbooks (Reingold, p. 10).

This book of clavier pieces must have been a great gift of magical dreams to the curious, ten-year-old Johann Sebastian. Yet despite all his pleading, his brother remained firm and Johann Sebastian never gained permission to use it. In the last decades of the seventeenth century, few music manuscripts existed in print. It was accepted practice to borrow a manuscript from another musician and make one's own copy by hand, a long and tedious undertaking. To loan a manuscript to a friend and have it accidentally destroyed might mean never seeing the written composition again.

Johann Christoph may have felt the book of music that had cost him many months' salary too valuable to entrust to a ten-year-old boy. Yet Johann Sebastian, determined and driven, discovered through experiment that his tiny hands could reach through the grillwork where the book lay locked within. He could reach through the grill, roll the pages up (for, as usual in the seventeenth century, it had only a paper cover), and pull the book out. It wasn't long before he took the book out every night, when everyone else slept. Only one course of action existed; to copy the entire book. Because he did not have a light, he copied it by moonlight sitting beside a window. He copied for six months. Finally he had his own manuscript. He was twelve years old when his brother discovered what he had done (Reingold, p. 11). Although it would be considered an innocent crime in today's society, zero tolerance existed for a breach of discipline in Johann Christoph's household. He took the child's manuscript. It is possible he did not believe a twelve-year-old could comprehend the complexities of the difficult music. Little Johann Sebastian's sorrow over this loss became enormous. However, being of a good nature, ready to move on to higher accomplishments, he "got over his disappointment and eventually forgave his older brother. The Capriccio in E Major, one of Johann Sebastian's earliest compositions for the clavier, was dedicated to Johann Christoph" (Reingold, p. 12).

Johann Sebastian lived with his brother for five years, and his formal education continued at the school in Ohrdruf until he was fifteen years old. After that he left for Lüneburg, traveling most of the way on foot (he rode on wagons for only a few miles) because he had no money for any other kind of travel. At night he had to sleep outside under trees. But young Bach knew that if he were to continue his studies, he must go to Lüneburg. And because of his excellent voice, he had no trouble obtaining a paid position in the choir, the Mettenchor, of St. Michael at Lüneburg. A choir reserved for poor children, the Mettenchor provided Bach with free tuition and board. By this time he had traveled about two hundred miles from his brother's house. This was quite a distance in the seventeenth century, especially for a boy of fifteen on foot. His voice broke the following year. One day as he sang in the choir, and without his knowledge or will, there was heard, with the soprano tone that he had to execute, the lower octave of the same. He kept this new voice for eight days, during which time he could neither speak nor sing except in octaves. Thus he lost his soprano tones and with them his fine young voice.

Certainly the fifteen-year-old feared for his position and possibly imagined the two-hundred-mile walk back to Ohrdruf, where he would have to be dependent on his brother again. However, his change of voice turned into a lucky event. Recognizing the boy's

> ♪
> **Johann Sebastian Bach**
>
> **Born:**
> March 21, 1685
> Eisenach, Thuringia,
> Germany
> **Died:**
> July 28, 1750
> Leipzig, Germany
> **Number of Works
> Composed:**
> Over 1,000

musical genius, the cantor (choir leader) arranged for Bach to stay on as choir prefect, or head of the choir. In this position he would be in charge of the younger boys. Bach also received the position of choir prefect because of his unusual talent as an instrumentalist.

While at Lüneburg, in 1701, during his summer vacation, Bach, now age sixteen, walked thirty miles to Hamburg to hear the famous organist Johann Adam Reinken (1623–1722) and to Celle to hear a French orchestra. When the music ended, Bach did not linger before beginning the thirty-mile walk back to Lüneburg. According to one story, he was hungry and tired, having had nothing to eat since leaving Lüneburg. When he came to an inn, he rested on a bench outside. He had no money to buy food. As he sat there, a window opened from above and two herring heads fell at his feet. He picked up the fish heads and found a Danish gold coin, a ducat, in the mouth of each one. With this considerable amount of money, he bought himself a meal, and there was enough left over to pay for future trips to hear Reinken. (Bach never did discover the origin of his good fortune.) In fact, Reinken's skill as an organist enticed Bach (on many occasions from his fifteenth to his thirty-fifth year) to walk to Hamburg to hear him.

During the next two years, Bach walked the sixty-mile round trip to Hamburg many times. To him, the arduous, dangerous trip proved worthwhile. From Reinken he learned the northern German tradition of organ music. Also at this time, when he was about eighteen years old, it is thought that through Johann Jakob Loewe, the organist of St. Nicholas Church in Lüneburg, he was introduced to French instrumental music. Loewe had composed suites of dance music in the French manner, and when Bach questioned Loewe about them, the organist suggested he visit the court of Duke Georg Wilhelm in Celle.

The more Bach heard about Celle, the more he wanted to see for himself. He finally decided he would travel there. It did not matter that Celle was twice as far away as Hamburg, sixty miles one way. He wanted to hear this different French style of music, to understand it.

No one knows how Bach, young and unsophisticated, made his way into the court of the duke. It is not known whether he played in the duke's orchestra or listened in the audience, but the important fact is the effect of the new music on his own compositions. By traveling so far, by hearing music so sophisticated, he acquired a thorough grounding in the French taste.

Bach appreciated the elegance, polish, and rhythmic styling of French music. He also liked the art of embellishment, or ornamenting music with decorative trills and grace notes, delightful details never experienced by German ears.

During the three years Bach spent at Lüneburg, he heard the booming compositions of three great organists, the finest church music, the grandest French and Italian opera, and concert music. His varied background in music was far more diverse than that of all others his age, and although he was not quite eighteen, he decided that rather than go on to college he would leave Lüneburg and begin a career as an organist. He realized he was still a youth, but everyone who knew and taught him and understood his gift encouraged this move. He longed for his own organ on which to compose, practice, and perform.

When Bach heard that the position of organist had opened at the German town of Sangerhausen, he did not hesitate to apply. This position had never in the history of the city been held by a teenager, but Bach impressed the town councilors, who had been told by travelers from Lüneburg that the young man about to apply for the position was a musical miracle and a phenomenon on the organ. After an astonishing performance, the council voted to give Bach the appointment, but then they had to bow to the wishes of the lord of the town, Johann Georg, who was duke of Sachsen-Weissenfels. The duke merely had to indicate his preference for an older man (without hearing Bach perform), and this gesture rescinded the offer to the young Bach.

Thoroughly discouraged, and even though he could have stayed on for another year at St. Michael's, Bach decided to continue looking for different work. Frequent visits to members of his family who lived in Arnstadt guaranteed that they all knew him, and the councilors of Arnstadt asked him to be one of the committee members selected to test the new organ. After he played the new instrument his reputation brought him invitations to test existing organs or provide advice on new ones. If he liked the instrument he would play for a long time, ending his recital with a complicated fugue meant to reveal the full resources of the instrument. Bach was young, they knew, but he was a Bach, and all of Arnstadt respected the Bachs.

> ♪
> **Interesting Facts about Johann Sebastian Bach**
>
> Some of his counterpoint compositions are so complex that few musicians in the world have conquered them correctly.
>
> When he was a teenager, he traveled 200 miles on foot, sleeping under trees at night, so he could get a paid position in the choir of St. Michael at Lüneburg.
>
> He was the first teenager to ever hold the position of organist in the German town of Sangerhausen.

When Bach impressed the town councilors playing the organ, they were also impressed with their new instrument, and they offered him, at age eighteen, the position of organist of St. Boniface's Church in Arnstadt. Now, he would be back in Thuringia, living in a town where many of his aunts, uncles, and cousins made their home.

No doubt the music of Bach's organ, the instrument he might have thought of as his own, filled the lives of the townspeople with pleasure as they went about their daily tasks. However, a major drawback occurred: He did not have time to compose. The town expected him to train a choir for the New Church of St. Boniface and a choir for the Upper Church. The boys did not want to learn, and not even the head of the school could keep them under control. Nevertheless the town expected Bach to mold the group of boys, many nearly his own age, into a sweetly singing church choir. He chose music he hoped they could perform and even composed a cantata (a serious anthem based on a narrative text) for presentation at the Easter services in 1704. The boys revealed their dislike of his music. This was the last time Bach ever composed for a choir. He had a quick temper, especially when it came to incompetent, ungrateful musicians.

Sometimes he found himself in trouble. One evening as Bach was returning from a musicale at Count Anton Günther's, a bassoonist from the church orchestra and five of his friends stopped him. Geyersbach, the bassoonist, threatened Bach with a cane and demanded an apology. Bach had reprimanded him during a rehearsal and had shouted that his bassoon sounded more like a bleating goat than a musical instrument.

Instead of trying to laugh the matter off, Bach grew angry, and when Geyersbach raised his cane, Bach drew his sword. He had to be restrained by the musician's friends. Bach took a month's leave of absence after this. He decided to return to Lübeck to see and hear the Danish organist Dietrich Buxtehude (1637–1707), one of the fathers of the arts of composing for the organ and the most important master of organ-playing of the time.

This time Bach faced a journey of more than two hundred miles, and he had to walk. But Buxtehude became extremely important in Bach's personal development as a composer. He brought drama to church music, a theatrical touch never before tried. Buxtehude based his music on biblical texts and successfully reflected the texts in his music. His composition techniques strongly influenced many of Bach's later compositions for the organ. Bach's use of tone repetitions, mathematical patterns as a basis for music construction, and his brilliant elaborate cantatas all point to the influence of Buxtehude.

At the time, Buxtehude, approaching age seventy and searching for a successor, knew Bach was his man. But Bach could not accept the position as organist at St. Mary's Church, although the position would have meant lasting fame and fortune. He could not accept because the man who succeeded Buxtehude would have to marry Buxtehude's thirty-year-old daughter. Bach was only twenty. He wanted the position and the security that went with it, but he was unwilling to sacrifice his personal life. He was young, he was romantic, and he was his own man. Also, Buxtehude wasn't Bach's only influence. The musician also admired north German composer Georg Böhm (1661–1733), beloved organist in Lüneburg.

In 1705, at age twenty, Bach took a month's leave from St. Boniface to become Buxtehude's pupil at Lübeck. Although he had no intention of succeeding him and marrying his daughter, it so happened that in the end he stayed for four months instead of one. Upon his return to St. Boniface, considerable bitterness over his lengthy, unauthorized absence erupted. The church council also objected to the changes in Bach's organ playing, calling his new style too theatrical, too dramatic and flamboyant. In four months his style under Buxtehude had changed completely, and the church council members recognized nothing of the old Bach.

Bach no longer accompanied church hymns in a simple way. He improvised between verses so flamboyantly that the singing congregation found it impossible to follow the melody that went along with the verses. Bach hid the melody with arrangements and accompaniments, which the congregation found highly annoying. They also criticized Bach's introduction of *tonus contrarius*, a tone that conflicts with the melody. They disliked the fact that he had not arranged music for performances intended for the voices and instruments of the gymnasium choir and orchestra. He considered their points of view and tried to compose to suit them. However, historians agree "[I]t is sometimes rather pathetic to see Bach involved in unavoidable clumsiness in the attempt to harmonize for Protestant church use" (Scholes, p. 621).

It was Superintendent Johann Christoph Olearius who has gone down in musical history as the man who complained vehemently about Bach's counterpoint, the main factor in Bach's musical genius. Counterpoint is the combination in one composition of many melodic lines, each with a rhythmic life of its own yet coordinating with other melodies to combine into a harmonious whole. It is the art of plural melody, and Bach was the greatest master of this art. His contributions to, and development of, counterpoint are the fundamentals of his genius. For this, and for refusing to work with mannerless young men in the choir, Bach was ordered before the consistory (church council) three times. Finally, he realized he needed to find a position where he could be himself and express the full potential of his ideas.

What had begun as a harmonious arrangement had become anything but, and in 1707, now at age twenty-two, he accepted a new post as organist at St. Blasius in Mühlhausen. Also, on October 17, 1707, Bach married his cousin Maria Barbara Bach. Together they had seven children.

Although only twenty-two years old, by now Bach was a settled young man. He had a wife and a position, and all he longed for was the freedom to be a composer and a musician in the way he knew best. Unfortunately, the congregation of Mühlhausen annoyed him as much as the one he had left in Arnstadt. They preferred plain church music to Bach's complex theatrical counterpoint. Priests hated his music. They considered all music, including church music, ungodly and worldly. If they gave a grudging consent to music at church services, the music played and sung would have to be insignificant. Bach's music was already (even at his young age) more elaborate and complicated than the simple songs and arias the churchgoers knew.

Within a year, Bach had requested release from this position because not only his music but also his religious views differed from those of his new employer. The superintendent sought to reduce concerted music, if not eliminate it, in favor of congregational singing. Bach worked with the more traditional Lutherans, who aimed at continuing traditional and modern concerted music. He had spent less than a year in Mühlhausen, and despite the incessant quarreling and criticism, he had, at age twenty-three, the fortitude, focus, and genius to write one of his most magnificent cantatas, "God Is My King." The town commissioned it for the annual inauguration of the town councilors, who egotistically believed Bach wrote the glorious music in their honor. The cantata is early evidence of Bach's consummate, mature genius. The councilors, inordinately delighted with the cantata, had copies printed at the city's expense. "God Is My King" was the only one of his cantatas Bach ever saw in print.

After moving to Weimar, Bach composed the Passacaglia and Fugue in C Minor. This composition, which is nearly impossible to play, makes such demands on the performer it is considered the ultimate test of an organist's skill. The form of Bach's Passacaglia involves the use of intricate mathematical patterns with a basic theme of fourteen notes grouped in twos, followed by a fifteenth note that returns the theme. In twenty variations on this unique composition, Bach expressed every possibility the theme offered.

Bach remained in Weimar for nine years. During this time, however, advancements took him only to the position of assistant *capellmeister* (chief conductor). Though Duke Wilhelm Ernst of Sachsen-Weimar admired Bach's work as leader of the orchestra and court organist, he did not make him capellmeister when the old capellmeister, Johann Samuel Drese, died in 1716. "It is true that the son had the title of vice-capellmeister while his father was alive, but Bach had often taken over the duties of Johann Wilhelm, a man whom Bach considered to be an inferior musician" (Reingold, p. 48). Bach knew he had not been given the post because he had previously disobeyed the duke. An angry Bach began to look for another position. Duke Wilhelm expected complete obedience from all members of his court, his subjects, and even members of his family. Today he might be called a "benevolent despot."

When Bach asked for his release from Weimar, Duke Wilhelm denied his request. When he applied again for a release, the duke, unaccustomed to such effrontery from a man he considered his servant, had him put under arrest and jailed on November 6, 1717. By December 2, with a grudging permission to retire from his service, the duke let him go. During his month in jail, Bach never wasted a minute. Working incessantly, he composed the *Orgelbuchlein*, or *Little Organ Book*. This is a collection of choral preludes based on forty-six hymns and is the dictionary of Bach's language in sound. If it seems amazing that Bach could have composed the *Little Organ Book* while in jail without access to a musical instrument, one must understand that Bach had contempt for those who needed an instrument in order to compose.

Bach's wife, Maria Barbara, died at the age of thirty-six. No one could point to the exact cause of her death, and Bach found himself with four young children to raise. A year and a half later he married a court singer, Anna Magdalena Wülcken on December 3, 1721. During their twenty-eight years of marriage, Anna Magdalena gave birth to thirteen children, only six of whom survived past early childhood. During his life Bach fathered twenty children, and several attained a high position in music.

Gradually losing his eyesight, Bach, at age sixty-five, underwent two unsuccessful eye operations in 1750. Finally his eyesight failed completely, and he spent his last months blind. To live in total darkness after such an active life composing must have been unendurable. After a brief six-month illness he died in Leipzig, Germany, at the age of sixty-five on July 28, 1750.

Historians conclude that Bach died in obscurity. The Austrian composer Joseph Haydn (1732–1809) visited the city eight years later hoping to meet the musician to whom his own music owed so much, but he could not find a trace of anything because Bach rested in an unmarked grave.

Bach lived in Protestant north Germany during the latter seventeenth and early eighteenth centuries when music existed for the glory and magnificence of courts, of municipal eminence, of religious observance, and of the daily happiness of the people. A persistent and tireless student of his art, Bach studied and learned even after he reached perfection. He gleaned whatever he could from other musicians. He stopped at age sixty-five only because he was blind and sick and unable to work.

After his death, the trend of musical interest moved so far from the fugue and the complexities of Bach's counterpoint, because of its difficulty, that his works went unperformed for years. It would be nearly one hundred years before enthusiasts revived his work.

Despite this great musician's achievements, the Bach legacy came dangerously close to being lost altogether. This occurred as a result of financial difficulties experienced by his widow and one son. They sold many of his unpublished works without regard to preservation. Also, Bach's musical style, difficult and nearly impossible to perform correctly, became outmoded.

We owe Bach's revival to the German composer and conductor Felix Mendelssohn (1809–1847), who inadvertently found a copy of Bach's *St. Matthew Passion*. Awed by its splendor, he organized a special chorus to perform it in 1829. Mendelssohn continued to glorify Bach and his music for the rest of his life. In 1850 the Bach Society was founded to publish his complete works. This monumental project took fifty years and filled forty-six volumes, but it finally gave to the world the magnificent music created by this unassuming composer who never stopped learning, never left Germany, and died insignificant and unappreciated.

Thanks to Mendelssohn's revival of the Bach legacy, Bach is now often called the greatest composer to ever live. Throughout the United States, Bach festivals meet annually.

Bibliography

Apel, Willi. *Harvard Dictionary of Music*. Cambridge, Mass.: Harvard University Press, 1967.

Reingold, Carmel Berman. *Johann Sebastian Bach, Revolutionary of Music*. New York: Franklin Watts, 1970.

Scholes, Percy A. *The Oxford Companion to Music*, 10th ed. London: Oxford University Press, 1978.

Schweitzer, Albert. *Johann Sebastian Bach*. 2 vols. New York: Dover, 1966.

Terry, Charles Sanford. *Johann Sebastian Bach*. London: Oxford University Press, 1962.

♪

Ludwig van Beethoven

(1770–1827)

Universally recognized as one of the most influential musicians in the history of music is Ludwig van Beethoven, German composer. His work crowned the classical period and initiated the nineteenth-century romantic era in music. The romantic school in music, taken up primarily by his fellow Germans, followed in his wake. Some historians consider Beethoven the first of the modern composers. He is one of the few musicians considered genuinely revolutionary.

During his fifty-six years, Beethoven composed more than two hundred musical compositions. His music spans a wide range of emotions. "More than any other composer he deserves to be called the Shakespeare of music, for he reaches to the heights and plumbs the depths of the human spirit as no other composer has done" (Scholes, p. 92). Personally he yearned for the title "tone poet." Because of this he cultivated within himself a profound sensitivity to be intense, passionate, and tender. He also had the mastery of music to express ranting, roaring feeling in the most tumultuous, blustery, and dazzling way. His frenetic genius surfaced when he was a child and ripened to perfection with age.

Beethoven was born in Bonn, Germany, into a family of pitifully poor, although truly accomplished, musicians. He was baptized in the Catholic parish church of St. Remigius in Bonn, Germany, in December 1770. His exact date of birth is not known; historians have yet to prove whether it was December 15, 16, or 17, 1770. At the time, the family lived in a cramped attic apartment in an obscure and dingy building in the Bonngasse. Today, the entire building serves as Bonn's

Beethovenhaus, or Beethoven House, with memorabilia and the Beethoven Archives, a substantial collection of research material.

His mother was Maria Magdalen Leym, and his father was Johann Beethoven. His grandfather worked as tenor court singer for the elector, or prince, of Cologne at the court at Bonn. His father, Johann, also an established musician and singer, later worked for the prince at court.

© CORBIS

Ludwig van Beethoven

Beethoven revealed talent far beyond the ordinary at an early age. It was thus that his father became his first teacher, instructing him at the age of four or five in both violin and clavier (an early keyboard instrument such as a piano). The child showed astonishing natural gifts for both instruments, and his father subjected him to an exhausting, brutal regimen with plans to display him to the world as a child prodigy. His father trained him with an iron hand to the point of excess and abuse, hoping to mold him into a second *Wunderkind* (infant prodigy) like Mozart.

Beethoven attended school for four years at the *Tironicium*, where pupils learned arithmetic, German language, and Latin. Mr. Wurzer, the president of the County Court of Coblenz and Beethoven's former classmate, later recalled that Beethoven did not listen to instruction. He spent his days half-asleep in daydreams, attended school disheveled, smelly, and sleepy. He seldom lifted himself above boredom.

Beethoven's family lived with another family, the Fischers, off and on. The Fischers said the child seldom played with other children and instead lived in his own private world of music, which he allowed no one to interrupt. Another earlier observer, Franz Gerhard Wegeler, recalled watching the sufferings of the child Beethoven from the window of a friend's house. He remembered Beethoven as a stocky little boy with rumpled black hair and penetrating gray eyes standing on a stool so that his fingers could reach the piano keys. He went through the exercises his father had given him over and over, tears running down his cheeks.

The child gave his first public performance at age eight, and by his ninth birthday he had surpassed not only his father's knowledge of music but also Johann's ability to teach him. After this, the father had to admit his son's need for further musical training from more advanced teachers. During the search for the perfect instructor, Beethoven endured a variety of training situations. At first his father arranged for lessons by the old court organist, Fleming van der Eden. As it turned out, the man had nothing to offer a prodigy. Fortunately the boy moved forward on his own, composing his own arrangements on the organ at various Bonn parishes. Quickly becoming accomplished, he played the organ every evening at the six o'clock mass in one or another Bonn church.

In 1779, when Beethoven was nine years old, a tenor singer named Tobias Friedrich Pfeiffer came to Bonn with the Grossmann and Hellmuth's Theatrical Company. Pfeiffer, a skilled pianist, befriended Johann van Beethoven. Upon hearing the man play, Johann decided that Pfeiffer should give his son lessons. Pfeiffer agreed. However, the lessons took place late at night after Pfeiffer and Johann returned home from the local tavern, noisy, drunk, and mean. Together they woke the boy, pulled him from his sleep, and dragged him to the piano for the "lesson."

Beethoven's maternal uncle, the twenty-four-year-old court violinist Franz Rovantini, became a more appropriate teacher and, among other things, taught the child how to play the violin. Whatever strides Beethoven made with his young and likeable teacher, the relationship ended suddenly when young Rovantini died from an infection in September 1781.

Thereafter the path of Beethoven's early childhood musical training turned even more unconventional. Apparently the boy's father realized he could not make money with his young musician by flaunting him before impressed audiences as a child prodigy. Therefore he changed plans and decided to teach his son to become a musical breadwinner and earn money for the poverty-stricken family. After this, "Beethoven . . . suffered from the tyranny of an unfeeling father" (Kenneson, p. 70), and he always resented his father for this. But at a deeper level he resented his mother even more. Weak and fearful, she listlessly endured her terrible marriage to an alcoholic and did not admonish her husband or do anything to help her son.

She may have been sick, suffering silently from deadly tuberculosis. She had borne several children, of whom by this time, in addition to Ludwig, only Caspar Karl (1774) and Nikolaus Johannes (1776) had survived. Her life within the home could not have been easy or even remotely happy. The family never had enough money, so besides her duties with the children and the household, she brought in extra money with needlework.

Beethoven did not attend school again. Instead, at age ten he became an apprentice musician at the Bonn court. Then, three years later, he took a job with wealthy Frau von Bruening, who hired him as a piano teacher for two of her children. As a teacher he liked his well-educated young pupils, and the three became close friends. In this circle of aristocracy Beethoven first read the works of contemporary German literature as well as some of the best world literature (English dramatist and poet William Shakespeare, 1564–1616; Greek essayist and biographer Plutarch, 46?–c.120; and other classical writers). At the same time he began tutoring the children of other well-to-do Bonn families. His work as a tutor provided tremendous financial help to his always-struggling family.

During the theater seasons from 1785 to 1787, Bonn's new elector (a German prince entitled to take part in choosing the sovereign head) Maximilian Franz brought a variety of opera companies to Bonn. Through opera Beethoven became acquainted with the works of the Bavarian composer Christoph Willibald von Gluck (1714–1787), especially his operas *Alceste* (1767) and *Orpheus and Eurydice* (1762). Also, Beethoven met the Italian composer and conductor Antonio Salieri (1750–1825), an associate of Gluck who instructed Beethoven for a short period.

Beethoven learned from Gluck and Salieri. Inordinately intelligent, yet at the same time a dark and dreary, sometimes slovenly person with little care for appearance or self-enhancement, Beethoven, deeply serious, had no sense of humor. Some might label his sense of humor different, as the following anecdote reveals. In the Catholic Church the lamentations of Jeremiah were sung on three days of the holy week. The organ could not be played during the designated three days, and therefore the chosen singer received only an improvised accompaniment from a pianist. Once, when it was Beethoven's turn to accompany on the piano, he asked the singer Heller, who exhibited complete confidence in his perfect intonation (that is, pitch or tone), whether he could throw him off. Heller wanted to participate, seeing an opportunity to show off his developed talents in pitch. Beethoven, however, wandered about so much in the accompaniment that Heller became completely bewildered. He could not find the closing cadence, even though Beethoven, with his little finger, kept striking hard and almost monotonously the note to be chanted in the treble.

While various members of the aristocracy gave Beethoven every favor and advantage, the chief organist of the court, Christian Gottlob Neefe (1748–1798), instructed him also. Beethoven had learned enough by the age of thirteen to become Neefe's unpaid assistant in an unusually highly responsible position. He became orchestral harpsichordist, a position that even included some of the duties of the conductor. The boy's talents were so prodigious that Neefe often left him in charge of the organ performances, even when he was only eleven years old, and early on predicted that the young child would become another Mozart.

As Beethoven grew older, those who knew him found him to be an upright and conscientious person. Friends found him, according to his inclination, happy and laughing or gloomy and depressed. He could be loving and affectionate or stormy and irritable. One month he trusted, and the next month he did not. He had a loud, boisterous, barroom brawl kind of laugh that he reproduced musically in a few of his scherzos. Overall, his nature remained kind and good, and his faults could be said to have sprouted from the seeds of his artistic temperament.

Beethoven's work goes far beyond the accomplishments of most musicians. The world's most extraordinary overtures and symphonies are among the nine of each that he composed. The world's most impressive pianoforte sonatas are among his thirty-two. The world's most unusual string quartets are among his seventeen. His Mass in D is powerful, and of all choral-orchestral settings of the text, only Bach's Mass in B Minor can stand on equal ground with it. He composed one opera, *Fidelio*, yet with only that one Beethoven made an indelible and impressive contribution to the theater.

♪
Ludwig van Beethoven
Born:
December 1770
(exact date unknown)
Bonn, Germany
Died:
March 26, 1827
Vienna, Austria
Number of Works
Composed:
Over 200

Perhaps he could have written more, but he did not write rapidly. He left piles of sketchbooks that have been studied so much his method of composing has been thoroughly researched. The overall impression one gains is that of a prodigious, inimitable individuality with painful difficulty finding the exact note, the precise course of expression. Only after Herculean efforts beyond those of any other composer who ever lived did his work rampage and storm into being. His influence on all classical composers who followed him evades measurement. Aside from his astonishing innovations and the expansion of the classical sonata and symphony, even as a young man he brought music to a cavernous depth, a theatrical intensity, a thrilling excitement, and a thunderous fervor copied by later romantic composers but never surpassed.

In 1787, at age seventeen, Beethoven went to Vienna, Austria, the most important center of music in the eighteenth century. Here he remained, according to some reports, for three months. No one knows who supported this journey, but some historians conclude that Beethoven had the elector's permission and a few letters of reference. Electors demanded unquestioned, complete obedience from their subjects. Few individuals traveled, and those who did needed permission. Records show that he arrived in Vienna in early April 1878. No firsthand reports or letters concerning his activities exist from his brief stay in Vienna. Therefore, one must be careful when reading the existing reports of his having played and improvised before Wolfgang Amadeus Mozart (1756–1791) and as possibly having received a few lessons from him. Some reports say Beethoven impressed Mozart, who took him as a pupil. Others say Mozart predicted that in the future Beethoven would force the world to notice him, to talk about him.

Most Mozart scholars agree there is no direct evidence that Mozart ever taught Beethoven. A story exists of Beethoven playing a well-rehearsed piece for Mozart that he praised politely. Excited by the praise, Beethoven asked Mozart to give him a theme. When the musician did, Beethoven then improvised so astonishingly well that Mozart supposedly ran out into the adjoining room. There, as the story goes, he commented enthusiastically to his friends that they should watch this young man, that someday he would give the world music to admire. A more reliable fact is that Beethoven could not have stayed in Vienna for even two weeks: While he was there a letter reached him from his father in Bonn telling him to return home immediately, as his mother had fallen seriously ill and might be dying.

Beethoven returned home via Munich and Augsburg. There he met one of the Steins (from the family who made the pianoforte). After an arduous journey he returned home in July 1787 and arrived just in time to witness his mother's final moments dying from tuberculosis.

Johann, his father, never recovered from his wife's death and sought relief from his sorrow and deep depression in even more alcohol. No longer able to sing, he could not earn a living. Thus at age nineteen Beethoven had to take over as head of the family. With great generosity, the elector paid the young Beethoven half his father's salary.

This amount provided Johann enough money to buy liquor, and he drank daily until he died in December 1789, nearly two years after his wife's death. In November of that year the elector sponsored

Beethoven, and he went back to Vienna. This time he studied with the Austrian composer Joseph Haydn (1732–1809), and during the two years he studied there, he earned a salary. He actually wanted the position as court composer at Bonn. However, when the French Army took over the city in 1798 and Napoléon became one of the leaders of the Directory, he remained in Vienna.

When he was twenty-two years old Beethoven decided to live in Vienna permanently. This seemed an excellent decision because Haydn had invited him to become his student. Unfortunately, after a few lessons Beethoven knew his personal relationship with Haydn would always be unsatisfying. The calm old master thought Beethoven's ideas were too eccentric, not in accord with the conservative, time-honored traditions he loved. The two masters never had open disagreements, but their meetings and all lessons ceased.

Both his breathtaking, unequaled piano virtuosity and his remarkable compositions won Beethoven favor among the enlightened Viennese aristocracy, and he enjoyed their liberal support until the end of his life. Out of appreciation for his music they tolerated his crude habits, his uncouth manners, his slovenly, unkempt appearance, and his nasty, outrageous temper. So beloved was he that no one questioned his magnificent compositions, no matter how bizarre or disheveled his appearance.

When Haydn traveled to England, Beethoven studied with the Austrian teacher of composition and composer Johann Georg Albrechtsberger (1736–1809), who had written a formerly important textbook on composition, an English translation of which remained in print for several years. Albrechtsberger, unimpressed by the young Beethoven, warned his other pupils not to provoke him but to leave him alone, not only because of his temper but because he was incapable of learning and would never make anything of himself.

After this, Beethoven descended into a period of dark monotony and found himself on the move from street to street, apartment to apartment. He remained within his regular circle of friends yet fussed and argued constantly, had bitter fights, and then did his best to appease his friends again. At the same time he reached the pinnacle of his genius and could no longer gain anything from instruction. While he suffered through these painful years, no one loved him. Although

Interesting Facts about Ludwig van Beethoven

He gave his first public performance at the age of eight.

By 1817 he was so deaf he couldn't hear the loudest notes banged on the piano, and he broke the strings on his piano in an effort to hear his own playing.

Scholars have yet to solve the mystery of the unknown woman, Beethoven's "immortal beloved," to whom he wrote letters that were discovered after his death.

he was in and out of love all his life with first one woman and then another, he never married. For several reasons he won not one of the women he loved. She was either married or of a higher social class or couldn't stand his unclean, coarse, and savage personal habits.

During the late eighteenth century, people recognized music as one of the distinguished luxuries of wealth and position in society. At this time, around 1798, Beethoven began to notice that he occasionally could not hear certain notes. Because he considered hearing his greatest faculty, in great haste and mounting fear he became even more prolific with his compositions. He performed more frequently before audiences. On April 2, 1800, he performed his first paid concert. At this time he produced his Symphony no. 1 in C Major and entertained the audience immensely with one of his piano concertos. Also, the Burg Theatre produced his ballet *Prometheus* in the following year, and it played for sixteen nights. A year later *Prometheus* had another run of thirteen nights. With deafness every day creeping upon him, he wrote the twin sonatas he titled *Quasi Fantasia*, the second of which was the famous *Moonlight Sonata*.

Three years later, 1801 saw the real beginning of Beethoven's deafness, an irreversible catastrophe. Deafness moved into his ears insidiously until, by 1817, he was unable to hear the loudest notes banged on the piano. Public performances became impossible. He withdrew from society and composed like a man loosed from an asylum. In his workroom in the old Schwarzspanierhaus he wrecked his Graf piano, breaking the strings in futile efforts to hear his own playing. One is able to note in old engravings his piano with strings snaked out and askew, broken by his banging on the keys with his fist. One sees his ear-trumpets. One also sees music scratched out, scribbled over, erased, crumpled, and discarded.

However, not being able to hear did not restrict Beethoven's genius or dampen his passions. One finds the creative outburst of his new, heroic style of composition in the Third Symphony in E-flat Major. The length, harmonies, structure, and orchestration broke all formal rules of classical music. Also different was the reason Beethoven wrote it—to celebrate human freedom. Composed in 1803, the Third Symphony, or the so-called *Eroica*, he dedicated to Napoléon Bonaparte, who symbolized to Beethoven the spirit of the French Revolution and the liberation of humankind. Later, in 1804, he decided against that idea after Bonaparte grabbed the crown from the Pope's hands and crowned himself emperor of the French in the Cathedral of Notre Dame in Paris. (French neoclassic painter Jacques-Louis David, 1748–1825, illustrated this scene in a huge painting, "Coronation".) Insulted and outraged by Napoléon's act, Beethoven renamed the work *Heroic Symphony to Celebrate the Memory of a Great Man*.

The *Eroica* Symphony begins in pattern (borrowed from an overture written by Mozart when he was a child), followed by several more gorgeous and fascinating patterns. However, even though they are extremely beautiful, tremendous energy permeates every one. Halfway through the movement one hears patterns shredded savagely. Beethoven, from the point of view of the mere pattern composer, goes insane, hurls and hammers the notes, and explosively batters and grinds them together.

Two years later *Fidelio* (or *Married Love*), his single opera based on a French text by J. N. Bouilly, played. It lasted for only three performances. Too complex for most musicians to play properly, it played the following year in a two-act version, The Prison Yard for act 1, and Florestan's Dungeon and a Courtyard in the Castle for act 2.

Fidelio, Beethoven's only opera, had its real beginnings in a true event. It tells the story of a wife's rescuing her husband from prison by entering it disguised as a young boy. The Spanish nobleman Florestan, hated by Pizarro, had been secretly put in the prison of the governor, his enemy. Pizarro had told everyone that Florestan no longer lived, but the nobleman's wife, Leonora, believed he had not died. Disguising herself as a young boy and calling herself Fidelio, she found employment in the prison as assistant to the chief jailer, Rocco. In this position she rescued her husband. Spring 1806 saw the restaging of *Fidelio*, which audiences enjoyed more politely this time; but the opera did not charm an audience as it would later in another revision.

Beethoven's long fascination with the text of Schiller's *Ode to Joy* found its reflection in the lines of the opera's final chorus, *Wer ein holdes Weib errungen*. The work unsuccessfully played in a nearly empty theater before an audience consisting only of Beethoven's friends and French military personnel. Beethoven later made a revision of the work.

King Jérôme Napoléon (Napoléon Bonaparte's brother) of Westphalia tried to induce Beethoven to become musician to the court at Cassel. Cassel's theaters always played to packed houses and invariably included the king on opening nights. The best companies of Paris and Vienna were regularly brought to Cassel. But Beethoven refused the king's offer, being already established in Vienna and preferring the enlightened, appreciative aristocracy congregated there. They tolerated his disheveled appearance, his notoriously crude manners, and his temper. Also, they agreed to pay him an unconditional yearly income to guarantee he would continue composing. He enjoyed their generous support throughout his life. Not long after this event in 1808, Beethoven (completely deaf) composed his Symphony no. 5 in C Minor. On March 27, 1808, he attended the final performance of the

Liebhaber Concerts at which the Austrian composer Franz Joseph Haydn, having a seventy-sixth birthday on March 31, received honors. Beethoven knelt before Haydn and kissed the hands and forehead of his former teacher.

In July 1812, Beethoven wrote letters to an unknown woman, his "immortal beloved." Discovered after his death, these letters left the world a mystery that scholars have little hope of solving. Possible recipients include Therese von Brunswick, one of his pupils; Antonie Brentano, the sister-in-law of his friend Bettina Brentano; and Biuletta Guicciardi. The "immortal beloved" letters, never delivered, lay hidden in a small private drawer in Beethoven's desk.

In the spring of 1813, Beethoven's brother Caspar Karl had his first serious, debilitating attack of consumption (tuberculosis). Later, when nearly dying of the disease, Caspar Karl signed a declaration expressing that in the case of his death he wanted his older brother Ludwig van Beethoven to have guardianship of his son, Karl. When Caspar died on November 15, 1815, Beethoven's life, already replete with complications, crumbled considerably. Beethoven and Caspar Karl's widow, Johanna, became co-guardians of nine-year-old Karl. Beethoven wanted complete guardianship of the boy and fought Johanna in the courts. In the end, he won and became guardian of his nephew Karl.

The young boy, however, caused him constant grief and anxiety. Karl's coarse and rude behavior added another impetus to Beethoven's gradual decline. In those bleak days of his life, Beethoven suffered from frequent and debilitating sickness and, finally, near-collapse from poor health.

Fortunately, inspiration came from the work of the Regensburg musician and musical mechanic Johann Nepomuk Maelzel (1772–1838), who became a friend. Maelzel invented a new type of clockwork musical metronome (Étienne Loulié, c.1775–c.1830 had already invented the first metronome, six feet tall, in 1696; Scholes, pp. 581, 613), basing his work on a principle formed by a Dutchman named Winkel. Maelzel also developed a new panharmonicon, a mechanical orchestra that fascinated Beethoven to the extent that in 1813 he wrote *The Battle of Vittoria* for it. The panharmonicon included flutes, clarinets, trumpets, violins, violoncellos, drums, cymbals, triangle, and strings struck by hammers. Maelzel also built an effective ear-trumpet for Beethoven (Scholes, p. 613).

Beethoven's popularity led the directors of the Imperial Opera to select his previously written *Fidelio* for stage performance. Beethoven and the German historian and theater poet Heinrich von Treitschke (1834–1896) revised the work entirely. They also planned a new overture. Beethoven began this piece but never finished it. On the morning of the premiere at which he was supposed to direct the final rehearsal, players found him asleep in his bed, the crumpled score to the unfinished overture scattered across the bed and over the floor.

One might believe the end had arrived, but Beethoven continued composing symphonies, concertos, and pianoforte sonatas. His battle symphony, *Wellington's Siege* (dedicated to the hero of the Waterloo campaign against Napoléon Bonaparte), honored the first duke of Wellington's most famous victory, the last action of the Napoléonic Wars, ending with the battle of Waterloo. The duke, Arthur Wellesley Wellington (1769–1852), had been a violinist in his youth and chose the last program ever performed at the Concerts of Ancient Music. As a benefit concert on December 8, 1813, *Wellington's Siege* played for a soldier who was nearly killed at Hanau, a town in central west Germany. The performance included the first presentation of Beethoven's Seventh Symphony in A, op. 92, composed in 1812. An unexpected and astonishing success, the performance, a powerful tour de force, played again four days later.

Between 1813 and 1820 Beethoven's work did not go well. He composed little. Unfortunate difficulties multiplied daily concerning Karl, his nephew. Most historians refer to this time, beginning around 1816, as Beethoven's final period. His last creations reveal turbulent emotion and intricate complexity of a kind one would not think possible. His works of the final period include the commanding, nearly symphonic *Hammerklavier Sonata* of 1818. His last works also include a late piano sonata, the distinguished Ninth Symphony (1817–1823) with its choral finale based on Schiller's *Ode to Joy,* and the *Missa Solemnis* (1818–1823).

By 1820 the world knew Beethoven as a great composer. As a person, however, most individuals found him unbalanced with aberrant ways, a slovenly anomaly with demented behavior and socially unacceptable manners. Some friends believed he had lost his mind. At the same time the inconvenience of his nephew Karl continued, with no end of childish harassment and ill behavior.

In 1824 (only three years before Beethoven's death), Karl failed his examinations at both the polytechnic school and the university. After the failures he attempted suicide, and Beethoven's alarm and distress became nearly more than he could physically withstand. Finally, Karl left Vienna and blamed Beethoven not only for his suicide attempt but also for his failure. Already weakened by the stresses of being responsible for Karl, the deaf and sick Beethoven, frail and disheartened, sunk lower.

It is remarkable that despite Karl and poor health, Beethoven still composed. Some scholars consider his last five string quartets, and the 1826 *Grosse Fuge* (Great Fugue), also for quartet, written during the last years of his life while totally deaf, his supreme creations, the pinnacle of his achievement. Music lovers consider the five quartets and *Grosse Fuge* some of the most beautiful music ever written and agree he saw the light of suns he had never imagined and heard in his mind the magnificence of melodies never conceived.

After a long, debilitating illness, Beethoven received the final sacraments on March 24, 1827. Two days later, during a thunder and lightning storm, he died. Legend has it he shook his fist in defiance against the thunder he could not hear and the lightning that threatened to set the earth afire.

Gillparzer, a little-known poet, wrote an oration for Beethoven's funeral. A sad and enormous crowd of more than twenty thousand watched the magnificent procession in which his contemporary, Austrian composer Franz Peter Schubert, served as one of the pallbearers. Schubert (1797–1828) had visited frequently the same coffeehouse as Beethoven, Bogner's Coffee House in the Singerstrasse. He would sit and watch the gloomy, irritable, solitary composer. Beethoven never met the man who adored him, and he remained unaware of the timid individual too afraid to approach his formidable presence. Schubert always watched the forlorn figure with the artistic temperament in the corner. It is fitting that he served as a pallbearer.

The large body of work produced by Beethoven serves as one of the most lasting and important contributions ever assembled by one composer. Through his work, classical music was revolutionized, its prevailing rules and traditional forms changed completely and forever. The ability of Beethoven's music to wring total emotion and the utmost awe from the listener transcended his own century.

A few of his contemporaries gave him up as a madman with lucid intervals of composing and playing. Others assert he used music as his personal way of expressing moods and got rid of the platitudes in pattern designing as an end in itself. Throughout his life he used old patterns with a staunch conservatism, but he imposed on them a flood of human emotion and passion. He not only played havoc with their symmetry but made it impossible to discern any pattern beneath the turbulence of emotion. He designed patterns with the best of all musicians. He arranged notes with a dark and stormy beauty that will last forever. He took the dullest, most ordinary themes and worked them into a cyclone in which one can always find something new, a grace note, an exhilarating pause, at the hundredth hearing.

Bibliography

Colles, H. M. ed., *Groves Dictionary of Music and Musicians*, 3rd ed., 5 vols. London: Macmillan, 1927.

Kenneson, Claude. *Musical Prodigies: Perilous Journeys, Remarkable Lives*. Portland, Oreg.: Amadeus Press, 1998.

Schindler, Anton Felix. *Beethoven As I Knew Him*. Chapel Hill, N.C.: Donald W. MacArdle, 1966.

Scholes, Percy A. *The Oxford Companion to Music*, 10th ed. London: Oxford University Press, 1978.

Thayer, Alexander W. *The Life of Ludwig van Beethoven*, rev. and ed. Elliot Forbes, 2 vols. Princeton, N.J.: Princeton University Press, 1967.

♪

Pablo Casals

(1876–1973)

In June 1950, the tiny town of Prades in the south of France applauded the public reappearance of Pablo Casals, at the time the world's most respected living violoncellist. Historians consider Casals one of the most influential musicians of the twentieth century. He was not only the greatest twentieth-century master of the cello but also an eminent pianist, composer, conductor, and humanitarian. Casals held an international reputation for a masterful, evocative technique that remains, even into the twenty-first century, unsurpassed. His eloquent interpretations of the German seventeenth-century baroque composer Johann Sebastian Bach's unaccompanied cello suites brought him worldwide acclaim.

In 1950, Casals came out of retirement to play and conduct the music of Bach in the remote French village of Prades, where he lived in voluntary exile from his native Spain in protest against the Spanish government. Fans listened to his music with appreciative enthusiasm. It had been three years since he promised never to play the cello in public as long as the dictator General Francisco Franco, leader of the Fascist revolt against the Spanish republic, ruled Spain.

Pablo Casals was born on December 29, 1876, in Vendrell, a Catalan village in Spain about forty miles from Barcelona. At the time, Vendrell had about five thousand inhabitants. The second of eleven children, nine boys and two girls, Pablo (or Pau in Catalan) Carlos Salvador Defillo de Casals was the son of Carlos and Pilar Defillo de Casals. Eight of Pilar's eleven children did not survive their infancy. Pablo, on the other hand, lived for almost a century. His father's family, all from Catalonia (Cataluña), an old province of northeastern Spain, can be traced to the sixteenth century. His mother, born of Catalonian parents in Puerto Rico, had one German grandparent.

From the crib, music was Pablo's love, and it became as natural to him as breathing. His mother said he sang in tune, and he sang by the hour, even before he could speak well. His father taught him to form sounds at the same time he taught him to express himself in words. A highly respected and accomplished organist in Vendrell at the parish church, he gave Pablo his first musical instruction. Early in his son's life, he noticed that Pablo observed and perceived with a rare and acute maturity. At age two, Pablo, on the floor resting his head against the Casals's upright piano, listened to his father play. He loved to stand behind the piano and name the notes Carlos played at random. He called them correctly for hours.

Carlos's warm, fatherly influence on young Pablo was considerable. However, his mother, Pilar, perceived Pablo's young aspirations to music in a different way. Throughout his life Pablo believed his mother, who was kind and full of energy, possessed a genuine understanding of life, a deep humanity.

Pablo Casals

When he was four years old, Pablo began singing in the church choir. In less than a year the choir taught him to sing plainsong (unadorned ritual music of the Western Christian Church). For his position as second soprano, even at five years of age, he received a salary. Also, he received eighty-five centavos (about ten cents) a night at choir rehearsals. Ten years later, as a teenager, he sang in his first real choir concert celebrating the 1861 Christmas Day *la misa del gall*, or Mass of the Cock.

By the time he was six years old, every new musical instrument Pablo encountered fascinated him. Also, by age six he had learned to play the piano. Even at so young an age, he played with ease the more rudimentary works of Polish composer Frédéric Chopin (1810–1849), German composer Ludwig van Beethoven (1770–1827), and German composer Felix Mendelssohn (1809–1847). Pablo's life changed completely, however, when he heard his father play Bach's *Well-Tempered Clavier*. After he heard Bach, every detail concerning the complex seventeenth-century baroque musician became Pablo's lifelong preoccupation. With eagerness and enthusiasm, and without fail, he began piano practice every day playing one set of Bach's forty-eight paired preludes and fugues.

Also at age six, Pablo started to compose and transpose music with no help from his father; that is, he wrote and played his compositions in a different key. With little difficulty he put together a mazurka (a lively Polish dance, like the polka). This charming composition he played for his grandfather, who, extremely pleased and recognizing his grandson's talent, gave him a ten-sous coin and several figs.

At age seven, Pablo played the violin, and after practicing for nearly a year he performed one of his favorite compositions in public. He played an air (a melody with a flowing character) that included variations (the main tune presented with many changes) by Jean Baptiste Charles Dancla (1817–1907). Dancla, a prominent violinist of the traditional French school and a respected composer for his instrument, also wrote several books. Musicians found his studies concise and immaculately presented, and his books became known and widely distributed at the time. His precise, well-ordered, seemingly simple compositions were the perfect choice for Pablo.

Equally important, Pablo and his father wrote music for a Christmas Day presentation of *The Adoration of the Shepherds*, a church play presented in 1833. Church officials asked Pablo's father to write background music for a few selected episodes. Having accepted the request a few months before Christmas, when the time actually arrived to write, he was too busy to compose so he asked his seven-year-old son to help. When Pablo began composing, Carlos watched him draw musical signs and notes on the staff accurately and with the assurance of an accomplished, well-trained adult. The compositions, all beyond exception, received high praise and recognition.

Pablo's enthusiasm moved to the music produced by many instruments, among them the organ. He desired more than anything from age six until he reached his ninth birthday to play the organ. He would sit on the bench with his father as Carlos played in church, and frequently he asked his father to teach him. He could not begin playing the organ, Carlos pointed out, until his legs were long enough to play the pedals. Finally, at age seven with his legs long enough, his father taught him the rudiments of the organ; and after several months, when his father had other duties, Pablo substituted for him at church services. His playing pleased the congregation immensely.

In 1885 Pablo admired a group of traveling entertainers performing in the Vendrell plaza. Dressed as clowns they called themselves Los Tres Bemoles (The Three Flats). Besides mandolins, bells, and guitars, they played other unusual instruments made from cigar boxes, washtubs, and common household items. Pablo watched a man playing a one-stringed instrument put together from an ordinary broomstick. Sitting in the front row, Pablo found himself entranced by the strange music produced by the broomstick. The man explained the one-string broom to Pablo, who told his father about it. "A few days later his father built him a similar instrument, using a dried gourd as a sounding board. This gourd-cello exists to this day" (Kenneson, p. 94).

At first Pablo played scales, then Schubert's Serenade. On his one-string gourd-cello he practiced until he could play compositions written by his father, and he taught himself the street tunes he heard every day. He worked diligently on his instrument and became so accomplished that one night he performed alone. He took his one-string gourd-cello to the old crumbling Santas Creus Monastery near Vendrell and gave a performance. "When he revisited the site thirty years later, he met an old innkeeper who recalled this childhood performance: 'An old innkeeper remembered me as a boy of nine playing my queer instrument in one of the cloisters'" (Kenneson, p. 94).

In 1888, Pablo, eleven years old, heard a real cello for the first time. A Barcelona chamber music trio performed at the Vendrell Catholic Center. Josep García, a cello professor at the Municipal Music School in Barcelona, played. (Later he became Pablo's teacher.) Entranced, Pablo would have listened to García until he could no longer stay awake. That very evening, after running all the way home, he told his father that he wanted to play the cello. Even with his sincere excitement, his father did not take him seriously. Pablo's persistence, however, appeared in several unusual ways. One was the way in which he held his violin. Holding it upright between his knees, he pretended he held a cello. Carlos asked him to hold the violin on his shoulder, but Carlos had only to turn his head away and Pablo would continue with the violin upright between his knees. Carlos, realizing the seriousness of his son's inclination, located a small cello, purchased it, and gave his son his first cello and then gave him lessons.

At the same time Carlos did not believe his son could earn a living from music, certainly not from playing the cello. Thinking the boy had to learn a trade in order to make money, he asked a carpenter to take on Pablo as an apprentice after his twelfth birthday. Pilar, Pablo's mother, who did not want her son's talent squandered, disagreed. She felt so strongly that for the first time she opposed her husband, an astonishing and brave assertion for a late-nineteenth-century woman. Nineteenth-century women did not dare oppose their husbands. Fierce arguments followed. Because Pablo had shown enthusiasm for the cello, Pilar, recognizing her son's unique gift, wanted him to have lessons from someone other than her husband. The small town of Vendrell did not have a cello teacher, and she knew her son would lose the best time for learning, his youth, by staying in Vendrell.

Carlos knew his son's compositions revealed sophistication and an inordinate maturity. He knew the boy had become a masterly pianist and a skillful organist. He also knew that Pablo's excitement for the cello had not dimmed and that in fact it was flourishing and becoming stronger every day. Thus he wrote a letter to the Municipal Music School in Barcelona and inquired about the possibility of enrolling his son. The letter prompted a reply to audition, one of the requirements for admission.

During the summer of 1888, Carlos remained in Vendrell while Pablo and his mother traveled to Barcelona. Pilar's relatives in Barcelona agreed to let Pablo stay with them during his studies at the Municipal Music School. He was eleven years old. For the first few days, to support and encourage her son, Pilar stayed with him. After that she returned to Vendrell, where she soon gave birth to her ninth child.

After Pablo's audition for the director, Maestro Bodreda, the school accepted Pablo enthusiastically as one of the youngest of the school's four hundred students. Pablo's schedule included both cello and music composition classes. Terrified the entire first day of his classes, he remembered nothing his teacher taught. To compound the situation, he did not understand the homework assignment and was too afraid to ask about it.

> ♪
> **Pablo Casals**
>
> **Born:**
> December 29, 1876
> Vendrell, Spain
> **Died:**
> October 22, 1973
> Río Piedras, Puerto Rico
>
> **Founder of the first annual music festival in Prades, France, organized in 1950 to commemorate Bach**

After school he returned to the home of his relatives and in tears told his mother about his terrible day. For the homework assignment he had no idea what to do. That evening, he became desperate and finally decided to compose something original on the bass (the lowest part of the harmony) discussed by the teacher that day as an étude (exercise) in harmony. The next day, when the teacher looked at Pablo's composition, he appeared to laugh and cry at the same time. To Pablo's immense surprise, the teacher grabbed him and hugged him.

Pablo's studies became so intense that it wasn't long before he had no time to dream of his hometown of Vendrell. Frequent visits to

Barcelona by either Pilar or Carlos kept him in close touch with his parents. They supplied the news he needed of the family, his friends, and the countryside.

Besides counterpoint and harmony studies with José Rodoreda, Pablo studied the piano with Joaquin Malats and the reknowned Spanish pianist Josep García, also his cello teacher. Pablo had heard García in Vendrell and, benefiting from his instruction, studied with him for the next five years.

Josep García eventually became Pablo's ideal teacher. The young boy respected his music and believed he could find no better instructor. Still, times existed even during the first lesson when he disliked García's plodding, conservative music. Sometimes the master's overly prudent moves seemed to Pablo pointless, even absurd. Consequently, he one day began altering García's instructions a little in the beginning, then almost completely. Eventually the rewrites helped him create his own new, unique technique. It was in this way that when only twelve years old Pablo began revolutionizing cello playing. García was the last instructor he ever worked with.

At the end of his first year at the Barcelona Municipal Music School, Pablo worked at his first professional engagement as cellist at the Café Tost. For summer vacation he traveled to Vendrell, and his mother, Pilar, accompanied him to San Salvador. At the end of summer he performed in concert at Tarragona. Later, his mother pasted his first newspaper clipping into a journal. In this same album she put the several excellent reviews that followed.

When school began again in the fall, Pilar returned to Barcelona with Pablo, and near the Café Tost mother and son rented an apartment. At the Café Tost Pilar sat every evening at the same table with a cup of coffee and listened to the remarkable music made by Pablo and his trio.

Señor Tost, the proprietor of the café, recognizing the fourteen-year-old's extraordinary talent, took him to concerts. They listened to German composer Richard Strauss (1864–1949) conduct *Don Juan*. They attended a recital by the world-famous, Paris-trained Spanish violinist Pablo de Sarasate (1844–1908). It wasn't long before a choral society that met above the Café Tost made Pablo an honorary member. They named the society the Orfeo Gracieno. The Orfeo members even gave him a diploma. His first childhood bit of prestige was this diploma. A Richard Wagner (1813–1883) enthusiast named Fluvia, who visited the choral society Orfeo, acquainted Pablo with Richard Wagner's nineteenth-century German romantic *Der Ring des Nibelungen*. Along with this, he gave Pablo the scores *of Lohengrin Parsifal* and *Tristan and Isolde*. For Pablo, Wagner's successor, Richard George Strauss, a German composer who wrote independent instrumental music in the form of programmatic symphonic poems, became a fountainhead of inspiration.

When Pablo's father visited Barcelona in 1890, he brought a full-sized cello and gave it to his fourteen-year-old son. Pablo needed more music not only for his new cello, which provided him with renewed inspiration, but also for his Café Tost audience. During one of his shopping trips in a secondhand music store searching for new compositions, Pablo found an antique Grützmacher edition of the Bach cello suites written nearly two hundred years earlier. This treasure changed his life completely. It is a miracle that in a tiny secondhand music store Pablo first discovered Bach's unaccompanied suites for the cello. So difficult and complex were they that he studied and practiced them every day for twelve years (until he was nearly twenty-five) before he played one of them in front of an audience. While in the music store, after discovering the Bach cello suites he couldn't recall the real reason why he had come into the store. He only stared at the music, of which at that moment he knew nothing. Over time, and with practice, the Bach suites became his favorites.

Knowing that Pablo practiced the Bach suites for twelve years before he felt confident enough to perform them in public, one can understand that during every single performance in his career he suffered severe, nearly paralyzing stage fright. In fact, stage fright descended on him without mercy when he made his first Barcelona concert appearance on February 23, 1891, at the Teatro de Novedades. His presentation formed part of a benefit for the elderly comic actress Concepción Palá. He reported that "'[m]y head was going round, fear gripped me fast, and I said, as I got up: What am I going to do? I cannot remember the beginning of the composition I am going to play!'" (Kenneson, p. 98).

> ♪
> **Interesting Facts about Pablo Casals**
>
> He was bitten by a rabid dog when he was a child and was only saved by receiving sixty-four injections of boiling serum.
>
> During every single performance in his career, he suffered from severe, almost paralyzing stage fright.
>
> He was an outspoken opponent of Fascism, and in 1946 he promised never to play the cello in public as long as the dictator General Francisco Franco, leader of the Fascist revolt against the Spanish republic, ruled Spain.

Throughout his exhausting pursuit of perfection, this debilitating fear always occurred just before his first song. During the long course of his career, at each of Casals's thousands of concerts, terror gripped him with just as much torture as it did the first time he stepped onto a stage to perform. Furthermore, every day of his life the fear never lessened. After his childhood, morbid fear brought on long and painful angina attacks; and as he played, his chest throbbed. Never once, though, did he feel disheartened.

Pablo Casals felt the pains of more than stage fright. He suffered through his teenage years in a way different from most young men. He had turned embarrassingly and excessively emotional and sensitive, especially when compared to other children his age. He suffered unbearably during his parents' continuing conflicts concerning his future. Fortunately, Pilar, his mother, always stood behind him with tact and compassion when his spirit, sometimes uncontrollable, threatened his sanity. His father, though, never understood his sensitive nature and did not realize that his son lived on the fringes of fatal emotional disaster. Pablo's internal stresses reached a much higher note than those of an ordinary teenager's phase of adolescence. Suffering pain, sometimes unbearable, he contemplated suicide. Finally, nearly desperate, he sought peace in religion and purposely underwent a quiet time of praying and religious mysticism.

After leaving the Municipal Music School, every day Pablo would visit Barcelona's church of Santo Jaime, a brief walk away, enter the cool, dim interior, and find an inconspicuous corner where he could meditate and pray alone. Sometimes, right after leaving the church, he rushed back inside, unable to maintain the strength he needed for the work of his daily life. As time passed, Pablo viewed his visits to the church sanctuary as the only way to restore himself.

Living in an endless emotional storm, Pablo finished his study of music in Barcelona. His mother, knowing he had learned all he could at the Municipal Music School, and recognizing his genius more than ever, told him the time had come for a decisive move forward. Stymied on all sides, not really knowing how to proceed, she decided to use Isaac Albéniz's letter recommending Pablo to the Count de Morphy. Albéniz (1860–1909) was the Spanish pianist and composer and Count Guillermo de Morphy was private adviser to Doña Maria Cristina, the Queen Regent and renowned patron of music. Thus in 1892, Pablo, age sixteen, his mother, and his two younger brothers moved to Madrid, hoping to catapult Pablo into the world of music she felt he deserved.

Pilar gave Albeniz's letter to Count de Morphy, and Pablo presented him his portfolio packed with music he had written over the years. Recognizing the talent before him and anxious to hear the young boy's compositions, the count arranged for Pablo to play for Infanta Isabel, a knowledgeable and appreciative music lover. After Pablo's concert, Isabel so adored him that de Morphy took him a step higher to the queen regent, Doña Maria Cristina. He arranged a cello performance at the palace. The sixteen-year-old Pablo had written all the music presented, and during the concert he pleased the queen immensely. Without hesitation she gave him so generous a scholarship that the family remained comfortably in Madrid. At the Madrid Conservatory, Tomas Breton became Pablo's composition teacher and

Jesus de Monasterio became his teacher in chamber music. Both musicians were worthy of Pablo's talent. Holding the highest esteem for Monasterio, an elegant man, Pablo called him the greatest teacher he had ever known. All of Monasterio's students became loyal followers because the kind master taught in an accomplished, sincere manner.

Pablo's personal academic education, however, remained in the hands of the Count de Morphy. The count nurtured the boy with every opportunity for success. He provided him extensive lessons on culture and manners at his home every morning seven days a week. In order that Pablo could express his thoughts positively and incisively, he made sure the boy observed and learned to appreciate the work of the greatest painters and sculptors Madrid had to offer. Once a week he sent him to the Prado Museum in Madrid, where Spain's best instructors helped him view and study historically the hundreds of paintings displayed. The count also saw that Pablo went to the classical theater to understand the most professional performances of the world's great plays. He sent him to the chamber of deputies to hear the words of the most famous speakers of the world. Every day Pablo lunched with Count de Morphy, and at the same time he learned the finest manners. After lunch Pablo entertained and calmed the busy count on the piano with his own compositions performed in the drawing room. Besides this, every week when Pablo went to the palace to play his own masterworks on the cello, the queen, a difficult woman with whom to find an audience, received him enthusiastically.

The Count de Morphy, highly regarded as a musician, had studied under the Belgian composer François Gevaert (1828–1908) and the Belgian theoretician, historian, and critic François-Joseph Fétis (1784–1871). He held views on music that accomplished musicians praised and believed significant. Pablo had lived in Madrid for only two years when Count de Morphy began speaking of him before audiences of scholarly musicians as the future composer of Spain. Pablo's mother, however, did not see her son in this role. She knew that if Pablo actually had talent as a composer, and she believed he did, the cello would never stop him. Also, as ever, understanding the brevity of youth, she knew that if her son gave up or neglected his cello, he would never make up the time lost.

The Count de Morphy and Pilar's disagreements over Pablo's future became so vehement that Pilar told him she would take Pablo and her family back to Barcelona. Because the count did not want to see Pablo leave, he finally accepted the decision that Pablo would study composition in Belgium with his own former teacher, François Gevaert, who lived in Brussels. Count de Morphy never once believed Pablo would not return to him and thus provided a substantial allowance for the family. Later, noting the boy's remarkable progress, the queen herself paid for Pablo's living expenses.

When the family traveled to Belgium, Pablo's father never came to terms with the fact that his family had left Spain, the homeland they all loved. Then, much to everyone's astonishment, when the family arrived in Brussels Gavaert told Pablo he no longer gave composition lessons because age had overcome him. He advised Pablo to go to Paris, where one could hear the best music on the continent.

Pablo and his mother decided to make the trip to Paris, but as the family prepared to leave, Gevaert asked him to remain long enough to go for an interview with a cello professor named Jacob. Pablo went to the interview with Jacob the next morning, but he did not carry his cello. Once there, he sat in the back of the room. When he listened to Jacob's pupils play, he knew right away they did not play well. After the students finished and moved to one side of the room, Jacob called Pablo to the front and, offering the names of quite a few compositions, asked him to play one of them. Pablo told Jacob to choose because he could play them all. Thinking Pablo arrogant, Jacob told his class that this cello player already knew all the songs that had ever been written and therefore needed no lessons. The class laughed at Pablo. He then grabbed the closest cello and began François Servais's *Souvenir de Spa*, a composition far beyond the ability of most mature performers. Afterwards, in total astonishment and sincere reverence, Jacob took Pablo to his office. He promised Pablo the first prize of the music conservatory if he would enroll in his class. Pablo reminded Jacob that he had been made a fool of in front of an entire class and because of this he could not stay.

Pablo left Brussels the next day with his mother and brothers, and they made the long trip to Paris. When Count de Morphy heard that Pablo had given up the plan he and Pablo had agreed upon for Brussels, he became angry and blamed the plan's failure on Pablo's mother. At the same time, he stopped financing Pablo. The situation turned precarious because the family had no money without Count de Morphy's support, and the expense of living in Paris turned out to be more than double what they had imagined. After much indecision and suffering, Pablo had only one choice—to look for work.

After a brief audition, the Folies Marigny orchestra hired him. Pablo lived close by the Folies and could walk from the apartment where the family lived to his new job. He walked, carrying his cello, to take his place with the orchestra two times every day to save the fare of fifteen centimes (pennies). In the meantime, his mother worked at home with her other children. She sewed all day and usually at night for money to feed her three children and herself. Pablo's father, Carlos, seldom sent money from Spain, and when he did it was not very much.

Finally, crushed by hardship, falling deeper into despair every day, and unable to meet expenses and even eat properly, the defeated family returned to Spain. Once more Pablo had to search for work. In 1897 Pablo, twenty-one years old, was hired by the Municipal School in Barcelona to succeed the great García as cello professor. He played the cello in churches and became first cellist of the Liceo (opera) Orchestra. Still working hard and practicing as many hours as he could every day, he met the Belgian violinist Mathieu Crickboom and formed a string quartet. He also performed with Enrique Granados (1867–1916), a noted Spanish composer, in chamber music concerts and at his conservatory.

Eventually Pablo resolved his conflicts with not only Count de Morphy but also the court. In time all differences were settled, and Queen Maria Cristina requested he give a performance at the palace. Immensely pleased, after the concert she gave him a Gagliano cello and had him decorated with the high honor Chevalier de l'Ordre de Carlos III.

Still only twenty-one years old, Pablo appeared as a soloist with the Madrid Orchestra and performed the nineteenth-century French composer Édouard Lalo's (1823–1892) cello concerto with Tomas Breton conducting. After this successful performance, Pablo went to Paris. This time Pilar did not travel with him. Pablo's move to Paris marked the end of his childhood and his sheltered life. The move also meant the beginning of a long separation from those who had loved and cared for him all his life.

Pablo played the Lalo cello concerto at his Paris audition. In 1899 he made his professional debut in Paris at the age of twenty-three playing Lalo's cello concerto once again with the Lamoureux Orchestra. His career as a virtuoso dates from October 1899, when Lamoureux asked him to play the first movement of the Lalo concerto at his first concert of the new season on November 12, 1899. Pablo's debut in Paris as a soloist with the Lamoureux Orchestra reached the highest peaks of success, far higher than he could have hoped. Important engagements in the capitals of Europe followed. Pierre Lalo, the son of the French composer and critic for the newspaper *Le Temps*, described Pablo's enchanting sound and miraculous virtuosity. When Pablo appeared with Lamoureux on December 17, the conductor praised him with an esteemed award, the Knight of the Order of the Violoncello. He had set a precedent. When considering the twentieth-century violoncello, one notes "[I]n the twentieth century the influence of the Catalan virtuoso Casals has been important" (Scholes, p. 1084).

After receiving such acclaim, and realizing his influence in the world of music, Pablo Casals continued to live in Paris. In 1905 he formed a trio with the French musicians Jacques Thibaud, violinist, and Alfred Cortot, pianist. He also performed for many years with the English pianist Harold Bauer. They played successful sonata recitals throughout Europe, the United States, and South America.

In the spring, when he returned from his concert tours, Casals taught cello classes at the École Normale de Musique in Paris. Here, he worked with a few truly accomplished pupils. At the same time, he toured the United States in 1901 for several concerts with the singer Emma Nevada. He returned in 1904 to perform in his New York debut. Here, he played Saint-Saëns's Cello Concerto with the Metropolitan Opera Orchestra. Naturally, as time went by, Casals's playing improved. On his third visit in 1915, Austrian American violinist Fritz Kreisler (1875–1962) announced to the audience that the "King of the Bow" had arrived. From 1915 until his last New York performance in 1928, Pablo Casals performed for American audiences nearly every year.

After a long and impressive career, the time finally arrived when Casals felt that the cello alone no longer provided him with the sincere expression he needed. From his childhood, he had felt the true call of the conductor.

Therefore, when World War I ended, he returned to Barcelona to begin his own orchestra. Unfortunately, instead of the Barcelona he remembered, he found a bombed-out city unable to afford a symphony orchestra. Steadfast and hardworking as usual, he held auditions and selected the best players who came and began rehearsals. On October 13, 1920, after endless problems, the Orquestra Pau Casals gave its first concert. In the beginning public attendance remained low, but after hours of rehearsals and persistence and paying all the bills himself, Casals conducted an orchestra that drew large and appreciative audiences. The Orquestra presented annual fall and spring performances, and after several seasons attendance went up and the orchestra supported itself. Casals found enormous success as director until the Spanish Civil War (1936–1939) at which time the Orquestra came to an end.

One of Casals's main accomplishments includes the first annual music festival in Prades, France, organized in 1950 to commemorate Bach. In 1956 he moved to San Juan, Puerto Rico, and by 1957 established the annual Casals Festival. In 1960 he composed an oratorio, *The Manger*, to promote world peace, and he conducted it throughout the world.

When Pablo Casals died in Puerto Rico on October 22, 1973, he was ninety-six years old. He had been considered for nearly three-quarters of a century the most important and influential cellist who ever lived.

Bibliography

Blum, David C. *Casals and the Art of Interpretation*. London: Heinemann, 1977.

Casals, Pablo. *Joys and Sorrows*. New York: Simon & Schuster, 1970.

Kenneson, Claude. *Musical Prodigies: Perilous Journeys, Remarkable Lives*. Portland, Oreg.: Amadeus Press, 1998.

Kirk, H. L. *Pablo Casals*. New York: Holt, Rinehart, and Winston, 1974.

Scholes, Percy A. *The Oxford Companion to Music*, 10th ed. London: Oxford University Press, 1978.

♪

Sarah Chang

(1980–)

Asian American violinist Sarah Chang's spectacular performances include concerts all over the world, although her career, unprecedented and unparalleled as a young classical violinist, has spanned only a few years. During the course of her brief career prestigious awards have been cast her way, notably the $10,000 1992 Avery Fisher Career Grant, of which she was the youngest ever recipient. Just as impressive is the Royal Philharmonic Society of Music award, the "Debut," which she received in 1993. Also, *Gramophone* magazine named her Young Artist of the Year in 1993. In that same year she received the Echo Schallplattenpreis, a German award. In London, she was named 1994 Newcomer of the Year at the International Classical Musical Awards. Since early childhood, Sarah has stunned audiences throughout the world. Experts, when judging her, usually call her the finest violinist to pick up a bow.

> [W]hen violinist Sarah Chang appears on television, for example, first at age ten playing a recital in London, then later at fourteen as soloist with the New York Philharmonic, we can judge for ourselves the young musician described by Yehudi Menuhin as "the most wonderful, perfect, ideal violinist I have ever heard." (Kenneson, p. 36)

Sarah Chang was born in Philadelphia in December 1980 a year or two after her mother, Myoung Chang, immigrated to the United States from Korea. Sarah's talented father, Min Soo Chang, and her equally talented mother were children of long and prestigious family lines of nationally acknowledged Korean scholars, architects, artists, and musicians.

Sarah spent her childhood embraced by a loving family and surrounded by music. She listened to the world's most beautiful classics. Music during Sarah's earliest years aroused her curiosity, and before her third birthday she attempted to play her father's violin.

Sarah was born Young Joo Chang, a Korean name. But when her mother's teacher, composer George Crumb, visited Myoung in the hospital, he suggested the American name, Sarah. He made the suggestion because he believed the child might choose music for a career. He said the possibility always existed that one day Young Joo might want to perform in public. Myoung agreed.

Sarah Chang

Myoung began Sarah's induction into music as early as she could. Besides having her daughter listen to classical music every day, she started Sarah's piano lessons a little before age three. The piano proved easy for Sarah; loving music, she practiced for several years. When she turned her complete focus to the violin at age four, however, her ability to play and her rapid progress flew to the highest levels in a matter of months.

In the beginning Sarah took violin lessons from her father and, learning rapidly and thoroughly, performed in public one year later. So tiny were her fingers that her father bought a 1/16th-size replica for her to use until her hands grew. Four years later, at the astonishing age of eight, she made her debut with the New York Philharmonic Orchestra. Surrounded by musicians twice her size (she was small for her age), she exuded supreme confidence. Following that unbelievable accomplishment, her performance as soloist with the Philharmonic in New York at age fourteen left those music lovers lucky enough to hear her overwhelmed and speechless.

From an early age, Sarah had many opportunities. When she was five her father took her to the Juilliard School of music, drama, and dance in New York City. He arranged an audition with Dorothy DeLay, one of the most acclaimed violin teachers in the world. Delay, who had been teaching for more than forty years, had heard every variation of prodigy the world had produced. Yet Sarah's audition left her floored.

When Sarah began working with DeLay at Juilliard, she was the youngest student there. So remarkable was her work that in 1987 Juilliard awarded her its Starling Scholarship.

By the time Sarah reached her eighth birthday she practiced for two or three hours a day; however, her practice hours increased as she grew older. (At age four she worked for ten or fifteen minutes a day, then at age six about thirty minutes to an hour.) Her mother, watching over her, divided her time into small segments because she felt her daughter couldn't concentrate, when only eight years old, for three or four hours without a break. She also thought that along with music, Sarah should have a normal childhood (at least as much as possible).

Today, Sarah and her mother both understand that training and disciplined preparation are the foundation and structure necessary for performing on the stage at the highest level far beyond even her best, most accomplished colleagues. Also, because of the necessity of so many practice hours, Sarah has changed her routine gradually over the years. In her teens, practicing as a mature violinist, she focused on underlying foundational basics more than she did as a child. Her primary routine ranged from hours of supportive vibrato exercises (a tremulous effect) to scales and arpeggios (the playing of the notes of a chord in quick succession instead of simultaneously) and études (compositions especially designed to give practice). Over the years Sarah has discovered that exercises performed under an austere, rigorous, and loyal consistency give her the fully matured accomplishments that build the security she must have on stage. She does this because she loves performing. She says,

> ♪
> **Sarah Chang**
>
> **Born:**
> December 10, 1980
> Philadelphia,
> Pennsylvania
> **Date of First Recording:**
> September 1992

> You see, there's really nothing that compares to being on stage. I think that feeling is really addictive and so fabulous that you can't describe it. And once you're up there from a young age, you're completely hooked. And nothing else comes close. I love travelling, I love recording, but ultimately it all comes down to those 40 minutes that I'm on stage. It's pretty amazing. (Apthorp, p. R16)

The result of stern, substantial, and continuous practice for her forty minutes on stage is that Sarah handles her bow unlike any other violinist. She commands it with faster-than-light expression, dramatically, theatrically, in a way no other violinist has been able to duplicate. Other musicians have found her technique masterly, replete with authority and a momentum impossible to imitate.

Just as other musicians have performed under the most adverse conditions, so too has Sarah. Through broken strings, mistakes by other musicians (sometimes serious), fire drills, audience members' heart attacks, and off-stage noises, Sarah has always continued her performance. She has never stumbled over a single note or ever played an incorrect nuance. So concentrated must she be to reach her personally imposed plateau of perfection that to open her eyes and look directly into the eye of another person, especially one who might make an expression or blink, can be so jarring that if not for her discipline she might forget a note, blur a note, stumble over a passage, or forget the music. To hear the slightest noise from the audience, or to hear something not the exact way it should be in the orchestra, can mean disaster if a musician is not rigorously and completely conditioned. A musician needs to do what she prepared herself for almost mindlessly, and Sarah has taught herself to reach this state.

Sarah finds Finnish composer Jean Sibelius (1865–1967), a composer of powerful individual feelings for his country (nationalism was the inspiration of practically all his work), most difficult. His violin concerto, deep and substantial, not superficial or romantic, is one of the most intense and difficult works ever written. One hears in Sibelius the sounds and silences of long, white, polar winters and the joys of brief, diamond-brilliant summers (Scholes, p. 949). Every note must be interpreted the way Sibelius intended.

Sarah traveled to Finland when she was thirteen years old. She chose the dark winter season because it was the time when the master composed. She visited Sibelius's house miles into the glacial wilds of Finland, far from civilization. On the day she visited, deep snow and ice covered the forests, trees, and even the lake beside the house, completely isolated and white, quiet, severe, and serene. In this cold and silent, icy forest she imagined Sibelius creating. She imagined how his symphonies and the violin concerto came from this barren, perilous landscape where winter kills and all life suffers. Only after her visit did Sarah understand the composer's music completely, his intense, mystical love of nature, his brooding, foreboding melancholy.

Under the bow of a violinist like Sarah, the beginning of Sibelius's concerto is sparkling, shimmery, and glistening like ice. Withdrawn, aloof, and isolated, it glows in a place where it cannot quite be touched. So powerful are the notes that a nearly painful loneliness overcomes the musician when playing it. Gradually the music leaves the snowy quiet and builds to a heated volcano that eventually explodes. At this time, every musical instrument in the orchestra clashes in a cacophonous eruption.

With Sibelius in mind, one can understand Sarah's belief that certain music can pull a person into depression and that some concertos, some passages—slow, minor-keyed, and sad—penetrate deep into the mind.

Some musicians consider the Tchaikovsky violin concerto with its gripping emotional expression and radiant orchestral color even more difficult than Sibelius's work. At one time there were violinists who declared Tchaikovsky unplayable even for music-matured adults. Sarah mastered it at age seven, after playing Sibelius. She feels that if a musician has the basic skills and the talent to play Tchaikovsky, if she works on it long enough and has the right guidance from a teacher or a parent, she will perform without flaw.

As she has grown older, Sarah has had to make the change from complete dependence on her gift to a higher level. Classical instrumentalists enter this transition world after reaching a perfection plateau. Only those who have built an invincible foundation will move beyond the usual plateau reached by most gifted individuals and reach higher, more difficult extremes. When Sarah studied with Dorothy DeLay at Juilliard, and following that over the years received guidance and support from different conductors and orchestras, her support system became solid and enduring.

Sarah will never forget some early incidents. The story of her audition for the internationally renowned conductor Zubin Mehta, artistic director of the New York Philharmonic, is well known. At this time she was eight years old and had been studying the violin for only four years. Mehta had asked her on a Friday if she could play on Saturday, the next day. She was to appear as a surprise guest soloist. Mehta's orchestra had already rehearsed, whereas Sarah had had no practice. Even so, she consented to go on stage with the orchestra and perform. She played the nineteenth-century Italian violinist Paganini's Violin Concerto no. 1, and in doing so she nearly paralyzed into permanent astonishment every member of the orchestra. Such a tiny girl with the maturity of a highly accomplished adult with years of concert hall experience went beyond their belief. So stunning was her performance at Avery Fisher Hall in New York City that the audience, including members of the national media and concert impresarios, stood at the end, clapping and shouting approval.

> ♪
> **Interesting Facts about Sarah Chang**
>
> She played the piano at age three and began playing the violin at age four.
>
> Her fingers were so tiny that her father bought her a 1/16th-size replica violin for her to use until her hands grew.
>
> Her audition for the New York Philharmonic at the age of eight so stunned the audience, including representatives from the national media and concert impresarios, that they all stood at the end, clapping and shouting approval.

By now, the stage, the orchestra, performing, and all the intricacies of music have become an important part of Sarah Chang's person. No doubt exists concerning her stability and continued success in the world of classical music performance and recording. Through practice and performance she continues to record. One of her compact discs for EMI is Sibelius's Violin Concerto in D Minor and Mendelssohn's

Violin Concerto in E Minor, performed with the Berlin Philharmonic Orchestra.

Today, the public admires Sarah Chang for her masterly, thrilling technique. Impelling, exciting to witness, electrifying, and inspirational to hear, she handles her bow like no other violinist. Her talent has carried her far beyond most musicians—so far, in fact, that critics say until we understand prodigies, we will never fully understand Sarah Chang.

Bibliography

Apthorp, Shirley. "Bowing to the Inevitable." Electronic Library, elibrary.com 07-08-2000.

Borzillo, Carrie. "Child Prodigies: A New Generation."*Billboard*, vol. 107, 34, August 26, 1995, pp. 1, 112.

Kenneson, Claude. *Musical Prodigies: Perilous Journeys, Remarkable Lives*. Portland, Oreg.: Amadeus Press, 1998.

Scholes, Percy A. *The Oxford Companion to Music*, 10th ed. London: Oxford University Press, 1978.

♪

Ray Charles

(1930–)

Ray Charles's genius manifests itself in many ways. He does more than sing: He has been an arranger, bandleader, recording executive, composer, saxophone player, and more than anything else, a completely unique, imaginative pianist. Even as a child, Charles had an effective and creative role in the music of the United States. Born in 1930 in Albany, Georgia, he has had a long and successful career that spans more than fifty years.

Charles fought, suffered, starved, and surmounted unimaginable obstacles to become one of the most illustrious and important singers and composers of the twentieth century. No doubt exists that he is a genius, the Genius of Soul. The sweeping span of his music has exerted an influence on other important and successful musicians, including Aretha Franklin and Stevie Wonder.

Charles developed soul music by arranging blues and gospel in previously unheard-of arrangements. His youthful, fresh, unexplored notes, strange and extraordinary, have inspired musicians worldwide. His extensive repertoire includes pop songs, country music, and any kind of song he feels like singing and playing on the piano, usually with no preliminaries. When Charles sits down at the piano, the unexplored comes forth or the old is reborn, re-created, or brought up to date. Once he attacks a song, the music is never the same.

When Charles performs, he usually accompanies himself on the piano and only rarely sings with a band. He can sing "Georgia on My Mind" and other songs like no other person in the world. His unique voice conjures up all the suffering and richness of the distinctive black experience in America. With intelligence, creativity, ambition, and drive, he has never—even from the time he was a six-year-old child just gone blind—let any obstacle block his ambition or stand in his path.

In the 1930s, Ray Charles's mother lived in Greenville, Florida. This small west Florida town was formally known as Station Five, the fifth stop from Tallahassee on the Florida Central and Western Railway. A frail, pretty orphan girl, the unmarried Aretha Williams named her new baby Ray Charles Robinson, a name everyone changed to RC. Although Williams was Aretha's surname, everyone called her Retha Robinson because a man and his wife, Bailey and Mary Jane Robinson, took in the homeless girl and raised her.

Ray Charles

When Aretha became pregnant, the father of her child was Bailey Robinson, Mary Jane's husband. Because of gossip, Retha, as she came to be known, only age sixteen, was sent to Albany, Georgia, to have her baby.

Toward the end of September she gave birth to a baby boy. No birth certificate exists, but the baby, when grown, always declared his birthday to be September 23, 1930. After a couple of months to get back on her feet, Retha returned to Jellyroll [the black quarter just outside Greenville] with her son. She named him Ray Charles Robinson. (Lydon, p. 6)

After Retha returned, Bailey and Mary Jane separated, and Bailey Robinson, who at first lied about fathering the child, had nothing to do with raising the boy. Retha and Mary Jane, however, always remained close friends.

All her life Retha was weak. Some of her friends blamed it on giving birth so young. She was sickly and even at a young age walked with a cane. Retha and RC lived as the poorest of the poor in Jellyroll, a sandy clearing of falling-down tarpaper shacks. They owned literally nothing. Mary Jane Robinson, who did all she could for Retha and RC, became RC's second mother.

By his first birthday RC had a brother, George. Retha believed in strict discipline and ruled her little family with an iron hand. When RC and George were five and four years old, respectively, they worked at general chores, chopped wood, and hauled water. They went to church with Retha, where fiery preachers stirred souls who screamed and shouted in ecstasy. They stamped their feet to rhythmic tambourines and clapping hands. Sometimes Retha tucked her children into bed and told stories of big men, the Ku Klux Klan, hidden behind white hoods, holding fiery torches as they thundered through the quarter scattering like leaves everything in their path.

Even while they were small, even before they attended the town's segregated public school for colored children, RC and George showed signs of unusually high intelligence. RC, remarkably bright, demonstrated an inordinate interest in everything. Music especially fascinated him. He either played the piano or listened to the jukebox with his ear pressed against the side. A friend, Mr. Pit, taught RC to pick out a melody on the piano with one tiny finger.

One afternoon in the summer of 1935, George drowned while playing in a tub as they ducked under the water for a penny. A few months after George's death, mucus began to collect around RC's eyes. Not long after that, when he awoke every morning mucus glued his eyelids together. Over the next few months, RC's vision clouded. Every object blurred. Glooms and shadows rendered his life a frightening, foggy landscape. Retha took her five-year-old child to see the one doctor in town who treated colored people. Unable to diagnose the problem, he sent the boy to a clinic in Madison, Florida, fourteen miles away. The doctor there told Retha that the boy was losing his eyesight and no cure existed. Doctors later guessed that congenital juvenile glaucoma had caused RC's blindness.

Retha, only age twenty-three, imagined the horrible life a blind black man would lead in the segregated, racist South. Yet she knew she had to do what she could, and she never faltered. She kept RC at his chores and worked him hard every day. She let no one coddle him, and she would not let him feel sorry for himself. She strengthened him in a way that carried him throughout his life.

All the while she never stopped searching for help until finally she discovered a state school for the deaf and blind in St. Augustine,

Florida, that took a few colored children. Retha had never learned to read or write and could not fill out an application to the school. She knew her son would have to go to school if he was to survive, and she was so persistent and desperate that a man and his wife, the Reams, helped get him admitted. The state paid room, board, and tuition, plus train fare to and from the school in the fall and spring. Retha did not have to pay anything. She would put RC on a train, the conductor would keep an eye on him, and a teacher from the school would meet him at the station in St. Augustine.

The St. Augustine school, rigidly segregated, became Charles's home for the next eight years. The state gave him his clothes and his food. He was called "Foots" because he didn't have shoes and even in winter had to walk barefoot. At times, RC, barely age seven, didn't want to leave his mother, and Mary Jane wanted him to stay at home. But determined to have her child educated, she sternly admonished him to mind his teachers and do his best.

At the school, RC's right eye began to ache. It gradually became unbearable until finally the child, alone and with no family, no one for support, had his right eye removed in the school infirmary.

Rather than sink into pity for himself, RC bounced back with uncanny determination. By the time he was eight years old, he discovered his single grand ambition was to be "a great musician." Once he made up his mind, he never wavered from his goal. At the school he learned to play the piano properly. Thoroughly schooled in the classical European music tradition with the piano works of Bach, Mozart, Beethoven, and Chopin, he learned as rapidly as the instructors taught him. He easily mastered music in braille, a difficult task because one hand had to be used to "read" the music. But he worked hard every day and practiced relentlessly.

In the school RC became the kid who played the piano, accompanied the singers, and sang popular songs to entertain his friends. After the first Christmas, when RC lived alone in a blind world on a nearly empty campus, lonely with no one close by who loved him, the staff donated money for his trips home over the holidays. After that he traveled back to Greenville every summer.

At the school, however, during the year, he lived in his lightless world by himself. He wanted to play with the other children, but they left him out of their games because he could not see. During these times he went by himself into the woods and cried. Sometimes, on the sidewalks of town he heard adults he could not see saying that someday he'd need a cane and a tin cup. Maybe these comments gave him the courage and determination that he used throughout the rest of his life.

His mother gave him these assets also. Defiant, always unwavering, firm and inflexible, Retha had no patience for self-pity for her son. Persevering, she told him education was the key to every door, that even if he couldn't see daylight, he wasn't stupid. That's why she had gotten him into the school. She told him he had to understand that whatever he wanted in life, he'd better learn to work for it because no one would give it to him. His mother's admonishments, her lessons on self-reliance, and his church became the bedrock of Charles's strong character. His sturdy foundation supported him in his climb to the top of music and entertainment.

As Charles moved into his teens, he never stopped playing the piano or singing or composing songs. At age thirteen he went to Tallahassee, Florida, and performed, revealing publicly for the first time his unusual, prodigious talent. Immediately he began playing the piano and singing with Lawyer Smith, Tallahassee's premier working jazz band for over thirty years. In Tallahassee the blind boy found his first taste of life and success as a professional musician.

So adamant was he concerning music that his punishment at school, when necessary, included being barred from the music room, a terrible fate for a child who practiced the piano many hours every day.

At school, in 1945, when only fourteen and a half, he stood five feet, eight inches tall and already had had more than his share of suffering. He had accepted his blindness and made himself strong. The day he received news that his mother had died, he crumbled.

> ♪
> **Ray Charles**
>
> **Born:**
> September 23, 1930
> Albany, Georgia
> **First Hit:**
> "Swanee River Rock," 1957

> [A] call came to South campus from Greenville. Retha had died; RC must come home right away. Mr. Lawrence and Mr. White found RC and broke the news to him bluntly. The boy felt struck as by a blow to his body. "Nothing had hit me like that," he recalled years later. "Not George drowning. Not going blind. Nothing . . . for a little while I went crazy." (Lydon, pp. 23–24)

Charles's mother died at age thirty-one. The doctor told the family a freak accident had killed her. A spoiled sweet potato pie may have given her food poisoning. Or, her death may have been the last chapter in an undiagnosed illness that had been pulling her down most of her life. A midwife, Ma Beck, told Charles his mother had spent her whole life preparing him for this day because she knew it would arrive. She left a philosophy with him he never forgot: to carry on, to keep going, to never give up. Retha had given him fortitude and toughness along with tenacity and an intense persistence.

Ray Charles has called the deaths of Retha and his brother, George, the two greatest tragedies of his life. His plaintive, mournful music tells the world how intensely their deaths marked him. The healing embrace of Ma Beck also later influenced the grown man's music and character. On the threshold of maturity, Charles was overwhelmed by sadness. At this time, the honest love of another human being touched him deeply. From these human experiences spring the empathy and understanding that vibrate throughout Ray Charles's music.

Retha never had the money for a church plot but (possibly knowing the end would come soon) had paid the Pallbearers' Society a nickel or dime a month year after year to ensure a decent burial. In the decades following her death, the Pallbearers' cemetery became a trash dump in the woods; lost under garbage, Retha's grave no longer exists.

After his mother's death, in September, Charles returned to school. He got into trouble almost immediately, and the authorities expelled him. Charles told the administrators they couldn't expel him because he would quit. On October 5, 1945, he returned home.

Only fifteen years old, he went to Jacksonville, at the time Florida's most populated city (two hundred thousand residents). Jacksonville's popular musicians tended to be black. Although laws kept Negroes out of most intellectual professions, black musicians could find work in music because of the appealing nature of their songs and lyrics. Recognizing this, Charles taught himself the songs people wanted to hear. Driven by ambition not only to enter this musical world but to conquer it, he practiced and practiced. Jam sessions he attended were close to kill-or-be-killed combat. Even a talented young man like Charles many times found himself flung out on the second chorus.

He learned one indelible lesson: Music was war. In fact, Duke Ellington called jazz musicians "gladiators." The music wars and the people involved hardened Charles. By practicing even harder and longer, he found the strength and ability he needed for competition. Blessed with a gift for hearing perfect pitch, he could hear the whole combo and each instrument's distinct voice at the same time. Blindness did not handicap him in learning song forms and chord sequences because all musicians visualize music's structure in the darkness of the mind's eye. Charles also had a natural aptitude for math, and this, too, gave him an advantage. Soon, the veterans couldn't throw Charles out of the song no matter what tricks they organized.

After playing with drummer Henry Washington, who held first rank among Jacksonville musicians, Charles knew he wanted a band of his own. Unfortunately, when World War II ended, the big bands ended also and a new style emerged: rhythm and blues.

Charles could not get enough of the new sounds. Everywhere he heard new bands. He idolized Nat "King" Cole. He had used Cole's work as inspiration for a long time. In his own unique way, he fit his piano accompaniment around his own voice in the same manner as Cole. Another influence, Charles Brown, helped Charles. Doing a slow Charles Brown blues was, for Ray Charles, simple. He could sing so much like Charles Brown that when just listening, no one could tell the difference. If Cole and Brown could make big money doing what they did, Charles knew he could make money with his music too.

Henry Washington liked Charles's Cole and Brown act and began giving him small featured spots with his rhythm section. People loved Charles as "Little Nat," and at age fifteen he felt the first stimulating hints of real success.

In September 1946 Charles had his sixteenth birthday. After only a year in Jacksonville, he had become a professional and even put together an act. It was after this that he went to Orlando, Florida. After a few weeks, however, the trickle of small jobs ran dry. For the first time, Ray Charles had no one. He was unemployed in a city where he knew no one and no one knew him. He had to make up his mind whether to stay in Orlando or leave. He decided to stay in the city on his own.

In the first months in Orlando, Ray Charles made no money. He slipped into desperation and became poorer than he had ever been as a small child. He went for days at a time with little or nothing to eat. He fell at times into the coma of hunger, and many times he could not focus. A scrounged can of sardines and a few crackers became a feast.

In Orlando, he learned that Bailey Robinson, his father, had died. Now Charles was truly an orphan. At this time it so happened that occasionally Joe Anderson couldn't get his regular drummer away from the pool table. Charles began to get an occasional phone call to help out with Anderson's band. He played in combos that performed on weekends south of Orlando in Kissimmee and north of Orlando

> ♪
> **Interesting Facts about Ray Charles**
>
> He started attending a state school for the deaf and blind at the age of seven, where he had to spend his first Christmas as a student alone on a nearly empty campus because he couldn't afford to go home for the holiday.
>
> He joined the premier working jazz band of Tallahassee, Florida, when he was thirteen years old.
>
> By the time he was fifteen years old, both his younger brother and mother were dead, and he was on his own.

in Deland. In the spring of 1947 he received a call to play in the Sunshine Club band. For this occasion he decided to compose a song.

In writing (none of which has survived), Ray Charles developed an aspect of his talent seldom noticed, but it is as important as the singing with piano accompaniment that made him famous. In his years as an unknown working as a professional, arranging became a marketable addition to his cache of skills, and in the 1950s Charles put together a signature small-band sound on his own.

By September 1947, his seventeenth birthday, Charles played piano for Charlie Brantley's Honeydippers. He also played with the Florida Playboys, a white country band. This interlude with the Playboys, though brief, planted a special seed in Charles's music that would lie dormant for a decade before sprouting. Then something else occurred when he was seventeen: He fell in love with Louise Mitchell, a pretty sixteen-year-old.

Soon after love hit him, Charles went to work at the Skyhaven Club with a group billed as the Manzy Harris Quartet. Harris, recognizing Charles's talent, turned the musical reins over to him and sat back at the drums, keeping time for whatever songs Charles wanted to play. The Manzy Harris Quartet had seen a little success, and Ray Charles became a recognized musician everyone loved to listen to. The Quartet lasted through the winter of 1948.

Charles made enough money to buy a 1947 Clarion model wire recorder. It wasn't long, however, before tape took the spotlight as a superior recording medium. Charles's earliest wire spools no longer exist, although he insists that a few are out there, released years ago on obscure labels.

In March 1948 Charles left for Seattle, sitting with other colored travelers in the back of the bus. Had he given up, Tampa, Orlando, and Jacksonville would have forgotten RC Robinson. Seattle, indeed, would never forget him. He and a friend named Gossie found success there, and that summer he sent for Louise. It was in Seattle that Charles began to wear sunglasses. They provided an instant glamour solution, and the Ray Charles façade became the symbol, known around the world, of an intriguing sightless singer whom no one could fully see. He was eighteen years old, handsome, dignified, and intelligent. He did not look blind. Unfortunately, he found drugs—marijuana and then heroin.

It was 1948, and after marijuana Charles used heroin for the next sixteen years. He drank and smoked even longer. Before he stopped doing drugs, heroin took Ray Charles to the gutters and nearly killed him.

In the late 1940s he cut his first record and had the thrill of hearing the record on local Seattle radio and watching it sell in stores. Still a teen, he released his first single record in October 1949 for the Swingtime label in Los Angeles, showing the vocal and piano influences of Nat "King" Cole and Charles Brown. At the same time, Charles was leaving his friends behind. Louise went back to Tampa, Florida. When she left he didn't know she was pregnant; the couple's daughter, Evelyn, was born in Tampa.

After this, in 1950, twenty years old, Charles went to Los Angeles. Again, he landed on his feet in a big new city. He met a woman named Loretta and moved into her apartment. In the beginning, Loretta's friends considered them married, but romance had died in Charles with the end of his first real love, Louise. Though he later married and stayed married for nearly twenty years, no woman after Louise ever completely captured his heart.

In Los Angeles Ray Charles began to live as he would for years, as a bachelor on the prowl, high on marijuana and heroin, making music and seeing women as he pleased. He kept no listed phone and no permanent address. He found the voice we recognize today when he signed with Atlantic Records in 1952. He stayed with the company until 1959. In those seven years the young singer changed from an ordinary musician to a person possessed of genius. He created warm passion and raw beauty in his music no one matched in the twentieth century. He consciously started to wean himself from imitation. This is when he found his own unique style.

Ray Charles at age twenty-five had turned himself into an accomplished musician. This was when, in 1955, rock 'n' roll emerged. Some give President Dwight Eisenhower indirect credit. His successful peace-and-prosperity era gave American teenagers money to spend and time to enjoy themselves. For the first time in history American teenagers felt less pressure to grow up and get to work. With "I Got a Woman" Ray Charles burst into rock 'n' roll, and the national consciousness enthusiastically recognized his accomplishments.

At the beginning of 1955, Ray Charles remained unknown to most Americans. Had he not forged ahead, historians would have listed him among musicians as a minor blues singer. However, by the end of the year, millions of Americans coast to coast recognized his voice and adored him.

Electricity powered rock 'n' roll. Cacophonous electric guitars unsettled every stage. No one played these guitars in the understated jazz tradition. They became eardrum-splitting, violent and furious. Singers turned up their vocal mikes to top the guitars. Before long, plugged-in basses and pianos roared hysterically. Musicians explored the tumultuous new timbres of unrestrained, thunderous electric instruments. Suddenly everyone knew Ray Charles and wanted to hear his music.

Although some people thought the extreme emotionalism of his gospel music and the earthy sexuality of his blues bordered on sacrilege, he gathered a dedicated following. He created one hit after another, soul songs he wrote and performed. In the 1950s his singles hits included "Lonely Avenue," "Hallelujah," "I Love Her So," "Night Time Is the Right Time," "This Little Girl of Mine," and the magnificent single that sold over a million copies, "What'd I Say." This was the beginning of Charles's successful concert performances.

Charles's most enduring and astonishing success, heard frequently even in the twenty-first century, was his recording of Hoagy Carmichael's "Georgia on My Mind" in his album *The Genius Hits the Road*. The National Association of Recording Arts and Sciences (NARAS) awarded him his first Grammy for "Georgia" as the best pop single of 1960 (Lydon, p. 200). Following this success, in 1961 and 1962 he released the two-volume *Modern Sounds in Country & Western Music*, which featured his personal versions of songs made popular by such singers as Hank Williams. On this album he performed the hit single "I Can't Stop Loving You," which sold two and a half million copies.

Subsequently, Ray Charles became the first black performer in history to find stardom as a country-and-western singer. "I Can't Stop Loving You" climbed the charts to the top with rhythm-and-blues and pop audiences. It remained at the top for fourteen weeks.

For four years, from 1961 to 1965, *Downbeat* magazine's poll of international jazz critics listed Ray Charles as the top male American vocalist. In the 1960s he visited many countries, including New Zealand and Japan, where his performances never failed to draw admiring fans and crowds.

By 1963 Charles had established his own publishing, recording, and management company, RPM International, and in 1965 he began producing his own records. He continued to write top hits up to the 1980s. He recorded *A Message from the People* in 1972, which included his inimitable, unforgettable "America the Beautiful." This version, powerful and moving, of a standard song released as a single became another hit overnight. At the same time, Charles won another Grammy in 1975 with his "Living for the City," by Stevie Wonder.

In 1990, trying something new and different, he used drum machines and synthesizers for the first time in his album *Would You Believe?* The year 1990 also found Charles in a television commercial. The story line: A prankster tries to fool Charles by replacing his Pepsi with a Coke. Charles can't see the Coke, but he can taste the difference. The New York advertising agency knew that using blindness for a joke might be questionable, but Charles, with his easygoing personality, smoothed over all awkwardness.

The 1990s also saw Charles holding eleven Grammy awards as well as countless other honors. In January 1993, he sang "America the Beautiful" for President Clinton's inaugural gala at the Lincoln Memorial. That October, during a White House dinner, the president awarded him, Billy Wilder, and Arthur Miller the National Medal of Arts.

Throughout his long career Charles said he never sought fame. He always, however, wanted to be the best at what he did. But now, no matter how many more hits he writes or sings, it makes no difference. Charles's place in the history of music has been established. He stands beside Duke Ellington, Louis Armstrong, and other legends.

Ray Charles was born a prodigy with a gift in music. His gift developed only because the boy and then the man let no obstacle stop him. Hours of practice day after day made him the best jazz pianist of the twentieth century. He trained himself to be a top arranger and songwriter. Extremely high intelligence enabled him to master the innumerable crafts of record making and the ability to run a business in a busy, political marketplace.

Ray Charles listened in the dark from the age of six. From his mother he learned not to pity himself, not to depend on others, not to take what he did not earn. And from everything he heard, from all the music he performed, he forged his own personal idiom and made himself more accomplished than any of his sources.

Ray Charles tells the world that one doesn't have to see life to live life. Though he might have strayed from his path occasionally, he reached perfection through determination and hard work.

Bibliography

Charles, Ray, and D. Ritz. *Brother Ray: Ray Charles' Own Story*. New York: Dial Press, 1978. Reprinted, Da Capo Press, 1992.

Lydon, Michael. *Ray Charles, Man and Music*. New York: Riverhead Books, 1998.

Ritz, David. *Ray Charles: Voice of Soul*. Broomall, Pa.: Chelsea House, 1994.

♪

Charlotte Church

(1986–)

Teenage Welsh soprano Charlotte Church's extraordinary, natural singing voice made her compact disc *Voice of an Angel* a million-dollar seller. *Voice of an Angel* went double platinum in the United Kingdom in 1999, where it sold two million copies within four weeks of its release. It reached the number four spot on the British pop chart and then rose to the number one classical spot. Church's vocal performances, although sometimes amplified, have made her an international celebrity. According to one review, "[Her] voice possesses enough dark, deep and sultry hues to charm a sphinx" (Bostick, p. 1). In the United States, *Voice of an Angel* made the charts at number twenty-eight, a phenomenon experts considered impossible for a complete unknown. *Voice of an Angel,* not only perfect in every note but also a soothing balm and lovely to hear, consists mostly of ballads and inspirational songs.

At age thirteen, on November 15, 1999, Charlotte Church released a second, all-new recording for Sony Classical, simply titled *Charlotte Church*. Highlights of the album include a new song, "Just Wave Hello," produced by Trevor Horn. On this recording her voice reveals a slight change, although everyone says it is an acceptable maturity. Also, her new songs have more than one theme and are not as religious as the earlier ones. "Just Wave Hello" is her first single. It came out in December 1999. Also in December she performed "Smash Hits Poll Winners Party" at the London Arena. The audience of eleven thousand girls screamed in approval and excitement throughout the entire program.

Born in Llandaff, Cardiff, Wales, Charlotte Church is the only child of James Church and his wife, Maria, a former civil servant who now manages her daughter's career. James, her second husband, adopted Charlotte in October 1999.

Charlotte Church first appeared on stage at the age of three and a half with her cousin. The two children sang "Ghostbusters" at a seaside holiday camp in Caernarfon, Wales. Even at such a young age, Charlotte felt comfortable on stage and loved singing before an audience. The power and sheer beauty of her voice astonished every person who heard her.

© Mitchell Gerber/CORBIS

Charlotte Church

By the time she was eight years old, Charlotte drew crowds at local karaoke competitions. Audiences young and old loved the purity of her voice, the naturalness of her demeanor, and the innocence of her songs.

Charlotte's career actually began one day in 1997 as she watched the *Richard and Judy* show on British television. The announcer said the show needed talented kids. Charlotte, alone in the house that day, phoned the television station. The skeptical producer told her that if she wanted to display her talent, she had to sing a song over the phone. With no experience or coaching, she sang "Pie Jesu." The television producer must have stood in his studio stunned and incredulous. Without hesitation, he invited her to perform on the television show *Talking Telephone Numbers*. Charlotte was eleven years old. Her parents did not know she had called a television station and performed over the phone; in fact, they were the last to find out.

Once Charlotte appeared on television, completely natural and at ease, viewers loved both her and her voice. This led to more and better television performances. Eventually her frequent appearances led to high-profile concerts at the London Palladium, then at the Royal Albert Hall and Cardiff Arms Park.

Sony Music signed her in 1998 after Sony Music United Kingdom chairman and chief executive officer Paul Burger saw her and heard her sing. Her voice and appearance left him so astonished that within minutes of her first visit to his office he had a five-album contract drawn up.

Charlotte Church found the worldwide success of *Voice of an Angel* a great surprise. The album sold six hundred thousand copies in the United Kingdom alone, and it reached double platinum status within weeks. After sales reached two million copies, Church became the youngest artist ever to have a number one album on the United Kingdom charts. The album turned gold in the United States about five weeks after its release. Church's *Voice of an Angel* album made her the youngest solo artist ever to achieve a top thirty album on the U.S. charts. This accomplishment won her a place in *The Guinness Book of Records*.

Traveling steadily, Charlotte Church has visited New York six times, Los Angeles three times (she made her concert debut at the Los Angeles Hollywood Bowl and received a standing ovation). She has had little time for rest, barely finding time to vacation with her family. *The Late Show with David Letterman*, *The Tonight Show with Jay Leno*, *The Today Show*, *Good Morning America*, *The Rosie O'Donnell Show*, and *Oprah* all have invited her to perform.

Besides this, Church has sung for royalty. In an astonishing performance at age twelve, she sang for Queen Elizabeth II when the Welsh Assembly in Cardiff opened. She sang at the Prince of Wales's fiftieth birthday celebration at London's Lyceum theater, and she performed at Pope John Paul II's "Christmas in the Vatican" special concert. Church's voice and personality so impressed Pope John Paul II when he saw her perform on Italian television that during Christmas 1998 he said he wanted to meet her. She went to Rome, met John Paul II, and sang for him.

Church has become known throughout the world. When she attends the performances of other musicians, sometimes she ends up being the performer. On December 31, 1999, she went to see the Manic Street Preachers, then went with her mother and father to their New Year's Eve concert. Before the band entered she went on stage, gave a short performance, and enjoyed herself tremendously, calling the affair the very best way to end the twentieth century.

♪
Charlotte Church

Born:
February 21, 1986
Cardiff, Wales (UK)
First CD:
Voice of an Angel, 1999

♪
Interesting Facts about Charlotte Church

By the time she was eight years old, Charlotte was drawing crowds who wanted to hear her at local karaoke competitions.

At age eleven, she phoned a television station when she was home alone one day because she'd seen they were looking for talented kids. The skeptical producer told her to sing over the phone, which she did. She was immediately invited to perform on the British television show *Talking Telephone Numbers*.

She is the youngest artist to have a number one album in the United Kingdom.

Despite her extraordinary voice, Church is still a regular teenager with a taste for pop music. Among her favorites are Natalie Imbruglia, the Corrs, Gloria Estefan, and Catatonia. She has no desire to be a pop star herself. She accepts the fact that right now her voice is not appropriate for pop music. Instead, she hopes to pursue a classical singing career, intending to appear in Milan at La Scala in the title role of Puccini's opera *Madame Butterfly*.

Charlotte also loves to shop and sleep over with friends and classmates at Cardiff's Howells High School. Yet in order to sing, she must travel constantly. This means she misses a lot of schoolwork, so a tutor always travels with her. She feels that her education is just as important as her singing.

Charlotte Church has sold millions of albums and has her own fan club (PO Box 153, Stanmore, Middlesex, HA7 2HF, England) and newsletter (charlottechurch.com). She has made commercials for major retailers in the United States. Ford used her song "Just Wave Hello" in its most recent worldwide television advertising campaign. Today, her future spreads brilliant and unmistakable, a curtain waiting to be lifted.

Bibliography

Bostick, Alan. *The Tennessean*. www.thetennessean.com/backissues99/01/, Sept. 11, 2000. p. 1.

Briscoe, Joanna. "Cardiff's Little Callas." *Independent* 14 (November 1998).

Entertainment Weekly 23 (April 1999).

"Keep Your Eye on Church." *Music Choice* (April 1999): 35.

"Small Wonder." *People*. (April 12, 1999): 146.

♪

Bob Dylan

(1941–)

A towering creative force behind twentieth-century folk music, Bob Dylan has become the spokesman of the song-poet generation. During the latter half of the twentieth century, his folk and rock songs altered the world of music. His lyrics, sometimes caustic, condemned and roused. His poem "Talk" became an indictment of Soviet hypocrisy. Although he has received criticism in every form, his 1963 *Precocious Autobiography* brought him the most cutting censure. Undaunted, he faced his critics and his angers and wrote about hope for himself and for his generation.

Dylan played to the generation just becoming adults in the 1960s. He was what Woody Guthrie, the poet-musician and ballad singer of migrant workers, represented to the youth growing up during the Great Depression of the 1930s and World War II (ending in 1945). Although sincerely shy, a genuine enigma, a private person, Dylan became the spokesman for mid-century alienated, asocial radicals and artists. His songs rivaled (and most of the time surpassed) the best work of Guthrie and American folksinger Pete Seeger. Dylan became the moral sense, the true voice of the hip culture.

Bob Dylan was born Robert Zimmerman in Duluth, Minnesota, on May 24, 1941. He was the oldest child of Abe Zimmerman, an appliance dealer. His mother's parents operated Ben Stone Clothing Store. While still young, Dylan moved with his family to Hibbing, Minnesota, a formerly prosperous iron-mining town northwest of Duluth that had fallen into economic decline. His mother said this of her son, who, with his writing, seemed destined to leave and never look back:

"The poems Bob wrote at ten or eleven were a chance to 'make something'; he was not especially interested in crafts or model building. He wrote a great deal" (Shelton, p. 35).

On August 9, 1962, at age twenty-one, he changed his name officially to Bob Dylan. Drawn to music as a child, his first idol was the country-blues singer Hank Williams; the gospel-trained Little Richard was his second. Only ten years old when he picked up a guitar, Dylan taught himself to play and by age fifteen had mastered in his own unique style the autoharp, the piano, and the harmonica. He had also written a ballad and dedicated it to French film actress Brigitte Bardot.

Dylan found his greatest inspirations in the songs and ballads of Woody Guthrie, the American folksinger who died in 1967. Guthrie, too, had taught himself the harmonica as a boy. Dylan was also motivated by the Negro blues of Leadbelly, Big Joe Williams, and Big Bill Boonzy. Further models included the country western music of Hank Williams, Hank Snow, and Jimmie Rodgers. Dylan also studied the harmonica techniques of Sonny Terry and the silent films of English film actor Charlie Chaplin, and he took from them what he needed for his own style.

In high school he fronted a rock 'n' roll band, telling friends he wanted to become a professional entertainer even greater than Elvis Presley.

Dylan searched the world early in life. Highways beckoned to him so strongly that between his tenth and eighteenth years he left home seven times. He earned a high school diploma at Hibbing High School and a scholarship to the University

Bob Dylan

of Minnesota. Deciding to try the world of academia, he walked onto the Minnesota campus in the spring of 1960. He was nineteen years old. For several reasons, though, his university life veered off course in six months. After alienating his English professor and failing science class because he would not watch a rabbit die, he was expelled. Dylan's counselor at the university later described him as seeming lost, as being a real loner.

At age nineteen, Dylan announced his lack of interest in a career. A restlessness he could neither understand nor contain drove him to the highway. He left his home, his mother and father, and his brother in Minnesota for the last time. After he moved to New York in 1960, Dylan attained tremendous popularity; even the sternest critics recognized him as a gifted, intelligent artist. His charm and appeal were not in his good looks and unique music but in his perceptive expression of social and cultural issues of the time. He stood solidly behind the folk rock rebellion in popular music that began before his twenty-fifth birthday in 1965. His caustic admonishments against racial bigotry, poverty, and combat in his hit "Blowin' in the Wind," and in his other songs, reached well-educated ears. Graduate students sang his songs, copied his guitar-harmonica technique, and clamored to see and hear him.

Throughout California, Oregon, Washington, Texas, New Mexico, South Dakota, Louisiana, and Kansas, Dylan roamed. A carnival took him in, as did the Colorado Rockies: He sang in Central City, a nineteenth-century gold-mining town high in the snowy mountains west of Denver. After this, he headed east.

January 1961 found Dylan and his guitar in Greenwich Village in New York City. By February he was where he wanted to be—beside the man he called his god: Woody Guthrie. But Guthrie suffered from Huntington's chorea and was an invalid in a hospital in New Jersey. Dylan worshipped Guthrie and believed he wrote the way Woody would write. Guthrie taught him that all people have reasons for what they do.

In New York City, Dylan slept in subways at first but later moved in with friends on the Lower East Side. He frequented the coffeehouses of Greenwich Village and performed in some of them, where fans found his coarse voice appealing. With his personal performances of folk classics, he created a newly restyled bluesy interpretation of old and new songs.

While performing at Folk City with a magnetic stage presence he didn't know he had (his innocence made him even more appealing), Dylan drew the attention of the prominent and powerful New York columnist Robert Shelton. Only a few weeks later, Dylan signed a contract at Columbia Records with producer John Hammond Sr. Hammond predicted musical greatness for the twenty-year-old performer with the gravely, scratch-on-slate voice. Dylan had a naïve yet thoroughly seductive street singer appeal and a rugged, charismatic stage presence.

In 1961 he returned to the University of Minnesota, where he participated in a folksingers' meeting of the times, a hootenanny, and gave a performance of Guthrie's songs that charmed local critics. He didn't remain at the university, however; once back in New York, he met upcoming folk artists Bill Elliott and Dave Van Ronk.

Dylan wrote and performed approximately two hundred songs (all unique) written in country language similar to the songs of Woody Guthrie. His debut album, *Bob Dylan*, released March 19, 1962, did not silence those Columbia executives who had dismissed him as "Hammond's folly." Acting on instinct, John Hammond Sr., one of the great jazz producers, had offered Dylan a five-year contract without hearing him sing—an unprecedented move in the music world. It was in this manner that after nine frustrating months of being snubbed by the leading folk music labels (Elektra, Folkways, and Vanguard Records), Dylan received his big chance on a major label without auditioning. He was underage at the time, and in the morass of music politics, typical jealousies caused him to lose friends. On the personal level he was the kind of person who did nothing to irritate anyone; yet similar to other extremely gifted individuals, he sometimes inspired immediate hostility. Hammond had no jealousies and, recognizing Dylan for what he was, made the best possible move by never putting any "strings attached" rules on him.

During April 1962, Dylan, only twenty-one years old, lived up to Hammond's beliefs when he wrote "Blowin' in the Wind," his personal petition for compassion and kindness that nearly overnight became the most influential folk song of the twentieth century. In June 1963, the singing group Peter, Paul, and Mary recorded "Blowin' in the Wind," and the record became the fastest-selling single in the history of Warner Brothers Records. So influential was the song that within months it became the unofficial anthem of the civil rights movement in the South.

The year 1962 saw Dylan writing without cease. He would read an article in the newspaper or see an image on television or hear a conversation and write a winning song. During the following year his work became more profound. He composed great twentieth-century generation-defining songs such as "A Hard Rain's A-Gonna Fall," "Only a Pawn in Their Game," and "Masters of War." Simultaneously and with new intimacy, he wrote several love songs.

He was twenty-two years old when folk singer Joan Baez boosted his popularity as a performer by inviting him onstage to sing at several of her concerts. Their performances together at the 1963 Newport Folk Festival before an audience of forty-six thousand changed Dylan's image from hobo-minstrel to poet-visionary-hero. It seemed he had suddenly realized the full potential of his genius and decided to use it. After this, with adept understanding and skill, Dylan influenced the youth of America.

Before he was twenty-five years old, Dylan released three albums of towering influence: *The Freewheelin' Bob Dylan* in 1963, *The Times They Are A-Changin'* in 1964, and *Another Side of Bob Dylan* in 1964. *Freewheelin'* was his first album to include all original compositions. *The Times They Are A-Changin'* was a powerful collection of stark social protest numbers that established Dylan as twentieth-century spokesman for the emerging generation of rebellious, intelligent, politically engaged, and enraged young people. *Another Side of Bob Dylan* consisted entirely of inward-looking songs replete with poetic images and personal statements of unusual intensity.

But the time came when Dylan no longer forged ahead with the work that had brought him success. He even argued that his protest songs, shrewd and successful efforts, proved only that the news can sell. This new Bob Dylan rejected the politics of the old Left, being the voice of the oppressed and the little man, in favor of a rebellious, socially subversive anarchism. At this time he wrote in a mystical-subjective idiom that seemed closer to the style of the English poet William Blake (1757–1827) than that of Woody Guthrie.

In 1965, when he was twenty-four years old, the year after the Beatles made their historic television appearance on the *Ed Sullivan Show*, Dylan, remaining true to the pattern of genius, changed completely again. He "went electric" and took on the mantle of rock 'n' roll. However, at the 1965 Newport Folk Festival, song purists screamed and hooted at him and his electric guitar and an electronically amplified backup band behind the stage. That era-defining incident revealed the unequaled power of rock music. It also foreshadowed the coming political split between the old Left, which had coalesced in the 1930s, and the new Left, the loud, destructive, rampaging, building-burning campus radicals of the 1960s.

> ♪
> **Bob Dylan**
>
> **Born:**
> May 24, 1941
> Duluth, Minnesota
> **First Record Album:**
> *Bob Dylan*, 1962

Consisting of acoustic and electric numbers, the 1965 *Bringing It All Back Home* album became Dylan's first gold one. This recording awakened the innovative wonder known as "folk rock." It displayed Dylan's new, highly personal writing style and his original, twentieth-century, stream-of-consciousness approach to lyrics.

Dylan married Sara Shirley H. Lownes on November 22, 1965. They had four children together: Jesse, Anna, Samuel, and Jacob. Dylan also adopted Sara's child, Maria, from a previous marriage. But the Dylan–Lownes marriage didn't last, and on May 1, 1977, Sara filed for divorce. Dylan's next album, *Highway 61 Revisited*, came out late in 1965. A world tour had exhausted him with excessive pressure. At this time he performed three, sometimes four, full concerts a week. Besides this, listeners demanded new albums and thousands of followers wanted new direction. Moreover, those on the business end of Dylan wanted more money.

In May 1966 he produced a double album titled *Blonde on Blonde*. Typically, Dylan's ideas changed again in this album. *Blonde on Blonde* begins with a joke and ends with a hymn. In between, insightful wit alternates with a prominent theme of the personal prison—by circumstance, love, society, illusions, and unrealized dreams. Most critics agree that *Blonde on Blonde*, along with the Beatles' *Sgt. Pepper's Lonely Hearts Club Band* of 1967, are the ultimate recorded accomplishments of rock music in the entire 1960s. *Blonde on Blonde* is a particularly high achievement, a superior collection that completes Dylan's first major rock cycle that began with *Back Home*.

As if unstoppable, he continued. *Highway 61* contains "Like a Rolling Stone," his only recording to rise to number one on the singles charts. "Desolation Row," one of his most ambitious efforts, and "Ballad of a Thin Man," one of his most popular numbers, both appeared at this time.

Dylan's method of composing always remained chaotic. He wrote and scribbled out and completed songs from roughed-out versions he brought along to recording sessions. For "Visions of Johanna" and "Sad Eyed Lady of the Lowlands," he suffered over a piano in a hotel room for five hours. "Johanna" is an instrumental work that cleverly draws the listener into a seven-and-a-half-minute masterpiece. A mournful mouth harp plaintively builds a sense of inconsolable grieving. Organ melody maintains the haunting melancholy.

Dylan's career reached a pinnacle in 1966 when he was twenty-five years old. By this time he had forged a second career in rock 'n' roll and had reached the crowning point as the most significant figure in twentieth-century rock history. Because he wrote his own songs, most historians agree his reign was far more impressive and powerful than that of Elvis Presley.

An important concert, Dylan's Paris Olympia performance, occurred on the day of his twenty-fifth birthday, May 24. Two thousand seats sold out more than a month before the concert. Recognized Paris critics compared Dylan to the important and influential French symbolist poet Rimbaud (1854–1891) and to the world-class French novelist Marcel Proust (1871–1922). They compared him to American film actor James Dean (1931–1955), French lyric poet (banished from Paris in 1463) François Villon (1431–?), and even the great Greek epic poet Homer (c. ninth century). The French loved Dylan not only for his total commitment to peace but also for his unique style of writing. They called him an authentic poet and the only true writer of the day. His haunting "Desolation Row" left an indelible impression.

Dylan spent the winter and spring of his twenty-fifth year on a tour, playing rock music with the best backup group of his career, the Hawks, a troupe of veteran rockers who later achieved fame as The Band. But Dylan had been using drugs for a few years, and his friends feared he was heading toward a death trip. In July he crashed his motorcycle, and reports circulated that he had broken his neck. Some accounts revealed he had sustained only minor injuries and used the accident as a pretext for withdrawing from the rock scene to cope with the excessive stress and pressures of life in the relentless public eye.

For a year and a half after the accident, Dylan lived in mystery and obscurity although he did not stop writing songs. He wrote, among others, "Tears of Rage" and "I Shall Be Released." He continued to perform privately at home with The Band. One day someone surreptitiously taped his music on a home recorder, and the tape meandered into the rock underground as a cult "bootleg" album called *The Great White Wonder*. (In 1975, Columbia released those home-recorded sessions as *The Basement Tapes*.) Meanwhile, Dylan kept an eye on the Beatles as they released "Sgt. Pepper" and the Rolling Stones recorded "Satanic Majesties Request." He also noted musician Jimi Hendrix, who adopted a different style known as "psychedelia," made popular through the use of extreme and cacophonous sonic distortion, bizarre orchestration, showy recording-studio effects, and uncommon lyrics.

In 1968, Dylan's response to his contemporaries was the album *John Wesley Harding*. It utilized spare and simple arrangements of acoustic guitar, bass, drums, and the occasional moan of a steel guitar whining through country-sounding parables such as "Dear Landlord," "All along the Watchtower," and the title song, "John Wesley Harding." Historians see the stripped-down lyrics as among the most impassioned and compelling of Dylan's career. Always in the lead, always the trendsetter, Dylan never hesitated in pointing the way to pop music's next big move; country rock. Indeed, Dylan's next album, *Nashville Skyline*, taped on February 13 through 17, 1969, was, like its predecessor, recorded in Nashville. *Nashville Skyline* produced a Top Ten hit, "Lay Lady Lay." It also featured a Johnny Cash–Bob Dylan duet on "Girl from the North

> ♪
> **Interesting Facts about Bob Dylan**
>
> Between his tenth and eighteenth years, he left home seven times.
>
> He failed a science class at the University of Minnesota because he would not watch a rabbit die.
>
> Despite his popularity, he's only had one number one hit on the singles chart: "Like a Rolling Stone."

Country." At a loss, some critics discussed what they could not detect on the album: no bitterness, no drug symbolism, no psychic wanderer. They said Dylan's voice was no longer the scratchy Dylan; he had added about eight notes to his range. No longer smoking, over time his voice gradually found new notes. Also, *Nashville Skyline* publicly reveals the private rapport that existed between Bob Dylan and Johnny Cash. The power and direction of *Nashville Skyline* soared beyond all dreams and expectations. Most critics agree that *Skyline* provided the link that brought pop music closer to country. In fact, the powerful influence of *Nashville Skyline* overshadowed the album. Even Dylan expressed amazement over the influence the album had on other musicians.

In the spring of 1970, Dylan accepted an honorary doctorate of music from Princeton University and took up residence with his wife, Sara (who he divorced in 1977) and children in a town house in Greenwich Village. After releasing *New Morning*, a moderately well received album, in October 1970, he again preferred the private life of a recluse.

For the next three years, Dylan released no new albums except in 1973. This was the mostly instrumental soundtrack recording for the Robert Altman film *Pat Garrett and Billy the Kid* in 1975. In the film, Dylan played a cameo role as an outlaw assassin. *Pat Garrett and Billy the Kid* seemed perfect for Dylan's film debut because the movie dealt with one of his favorite themes, that of the battle-fatigued antihero.

Dylan had such presence on the screen that the studio wanted the role rewritten and enlarged. Dylan, however, would not go along with the idea. His publicist let studio executives know how genuinely shy and withdrawn he really was. Critics followed him around, but he always managed to dodge them. The result was that they interviewed other people, trying to get information about the elusive star. With secondhand information, an inaccurate picture emerged. But there was no doubt about it: Without trying, Dylan upstaged even the director. The film became a cult movie, frequently revived at art houses. Dylan's sound-track album, a model of economy, was yet another trail blazed.

Early in 1974, Dylan emerged from semiretirement by releasing *Planet Waves*, an album of new material that reveals the multitudinous faces of love. If listened to as a trilogy with the two subsequent albums, *Blood on the Tracks* and *Desire*, the album can be said to celebrate even another new stylistic period and an innovative attack on language by a poet.

Blood on the Tracks included restless songs about remorse and loss, impermanence and fragmentation and relationships, the demons of love and death. Musicians and critics alike called *Blood on the Tracks* Dylan's best work to date.

Here the renewed Dylan reached fresh heights. Critical re-
action ran to superlatives, calling *Blood* the best Dylan work
in seven or nine years, or even his best work *ever.* . . . The artist
was in torment. One of his most listenable albums, musically
lustrous and varied, it contains some of his most direct, rich,
emotive, and supple vocalizing. . . . These ten songs show high
craftsmanship and control. . . . Basic elements—blood, pain,
storm, and rain—assume dozens of patterns . . . [and reveal
that] life is a battleground. (Shelton, p. 440)

After this, Dylan decided to go on a nationwide tour. His comeback
tour, one of the decade's most successful series of rock concerts, produced another highly esteemed live album, *Before the Flood*.

Dylan went on *Saturday Night Live* on October 20, 1979. Thereafter,
singing not one of his old songs, he performed in fourteen concerts
at the Fox Warfield theater in San Francisco, where audiences, demanding the old songs, hooted and jeered at him. On February 17,
1980, he won a Grammy Award for "Gotta Serve Somebody." Surprisingly, he accepted the award in white-tie formal dress. In 1985, he
received the coveted and honored position of closing the "Live Aid"
spectacular, which was broadcast for sixteen hours and raised $50
million for starving Africans.

Critics expected Dylan to fade and disappear. But in 1992 he released a collection of standard blues songs, *Good As I Been to You*, in
which he returned to his original guitar and harmonica combination.
In *Good As I Been*, Dylan speaks again about his past. He faced a different audience this time—young people, students, and fans young in
a way different from what he had experienced in the 1960s. What he
found was that they loved his music, the guitar and harmonica combination that thirty years ago had awakened the listening world. They
discovered that the more they listened to *Good As I Been to You*, the
more they realized that music has no age.

In 1997, Dylan released *Time Out of Mind*, and it was nominated for
album of the year at the Grammy Awards. The year 1997 also saw
Dylan in an October performance before Pope John Paul II.

During his life, Dylan has written verse and made music that has
influenced an entire generation. He has caused some to hate and others to worship him and his ideas. Very few have heard him and remained neutral. He's like a kaleidoscope of unlimited facets.

"There's so many sides to Dylan, he's round," said a Wood-
stock friend. . . . "He's a disturber of the peace—ours as well
as his own. . . . He's already poured five lifetimes into one. He
may follow Rimbaud's route, having articulated more of the

language of revolt than the world was then ready for. Or he may follow Yeats's route of more seeking and more finding and even greater creativity toward old age." (Shelton, p. 498)

Bibliography

Feinstein, Barry, Faniel Kramer, and Jim Marshall. *Early Dylan*. Boston: Bulfinch Press, 1999. A collection of photographs.

McKeen, William. *Bob Dylan: A Bio-bibliography*. Westport, Conn.: Greenwood Press, 1993.

Shelton, Robert. *No Direction Home. The Life and Music of Bob Dylan*. New York: Da Capo Press, 1997.

Williams, Richard. *Dylan: A Man Called Alias*. New York: Holt, 1992.

♪

John Lennon

(1940–1980)

John Lennon, founder and leader of the Beatles, created the group while still in his teens. As a schoolboy, then a teenage art college student, then a Beatle and solo performer, Lennon developed his gift that took music beyond traditional rock 'n' roll. Indeed, he marked the world with his music.

John Winston Lennon, named after his paternal grandfather, was born in Liverpool, England, on October 9, 1940, at 6:30 P.M. at Oxford Street Maternity Hospital. "[The] Lennon name is the anglicized version of O'Leannain, a clan found in the Galway, Fermanagh, and Cork areas of southern Ireland" (Coleman, p. 86). On the night of John's birth, Hitler's Luftwaffe bombed Liverpool and John was put under a bed in the hospital for safety.

In 1945, a social worker from Liverpool's social services department told Julia, John's mother, her home was not suitable for raising a child. Julia, a former cinema usherette, was not upset; she did not really want him. John's father, a ship's steward on troop ships during World War II, Fred (Alfred) Lennon, had deserted him and his mother when he was three years old. Fred returned in 1946 and took John to Blackpool. Julia, who didn't want Fred to raise the child, found them and gave the child the choice of staying with his father or mother. He chose his mother. His life to that point had been turmoil.

By [July 1946] John had settled into his aunt Mimi's home, [and] had suffered enough emotional trauma to cripple any but the strongest soul. He had been neglected, uprooted, passed from hand to hand, and finally compelled to make an impossible choice: either to give up his mother in order to retain his father or to relinquish his father in order to hold on to his mother, who, as it turned out, really didn't want him. (Goldman, p. 33)

Julia returned John to Liverpool to stay with Mimi, the adoring, no-nonsense aunt who raised him. "Even as a toddler John was defiant, determined, and a leader. When he played cowboys and Indians, in the garden of Mimi's home, she recalled: 'He had to be in charge. Always'" (Coleman, p. 96). However, rather than play with other children, Lennon preferred books, especially the *Just William* series by Richmal Crompton. In the world of imagination that books provided, he developed his own mischievous, witty, complex personality. He read and reread *Alice in Wonderland* and recited long sections. He read the difficult French novelist Honoré de Balzac's works several times. (The influence of Balzac, 1799–1850, is evident in his lyrics.) Mimi said later, "I thought there was a lot of Balzac in his song writing later on. Anyway, he'd read most of the classics by the time he was ten" (Coleman, p. 100).

John Lennon

Mimi sent John to primary school when he was five years old. To travel the three miles there, he rode a bus past the Salvation Army Hostel in Strawberry Field, down to Penny Lane. (Places he knew as a child made later appearances in his songs.)

Julia had introduced John at a very young age to music. She played the banjo and taught him a few chords. Within days, his interest in music became insatiable and he wanted a guitar. Because neither his mother nor his aunt would give him one, he contacted a mail order company. He purchased a nine dollar model, guaranteed not to split, from an advertisement in the *Daily Mail*. He had it sent to Julia's address and told Mimi that Julia (too busy to notice) had given it to him. In a few hours, he had worked out the chords to the Buddy Holly hit "That'll Be The Day."

Besides teaching him chords, Julia had also played for him the early Elvis Presley recordings, which John loved. Later, on Radio Luxembourg, Lennon heard Elvis Presley's "Heartbreak Hotel." Elvis followed "Hotel" with "Don't Be Cruel" and "Hound Dog." Both songs changed John Lennon's life forever. He said, "After that . . . nothing was the same for me. He did it for me" (Coleman, p. 134). The world had crowned Elvis the king of rock 'n' roll. Rude, gauche, and loud, he was skewered by the critics as a danger to morality. Aunt Mimi said John changed completely almost overnight because of Elvis Presley. He loved Elvis's look, his rudeness, his hip swivelling, the idea that when he spoke, which was rare, he mumbled. Elvis fueled John's suppressed resentment of authority. For the first time since Mimi had taken him in, he wouldn't let her into his bedroom. He became disheveled and disordered. Mimi called this time in his life (he was sixteen) his "Elvis period."

Lennon's talent went beyond music. In fact, he showed such original talent for art that the headmaster at his grammar school told Mimi he should become an artist. Because of this recommendation, Lennon, with the help of his aunt, attended the Liverpool College of Art for two years. He began his studies in September 1957.

At Liverpool College of Art, his teachers bored him. They reluctantly agreed he had talent, yet they did not notice his drawing. John took art classes, but even while studying drawing he never strayed far from music.

While American teenagers copied movie stars like Marlon Brando and James Dean by wearing T-shirts and jeans, in Britain the new look that became a uniform for teenagers was called the teddy boy outfit—so called because of its resemblance to Edwardian fashions. Greasy hair and side whiskers grown far down the face for example, became a major requirement of a ted. In 1958, Lennon, at age eighteen, wore these teddy boy clothes—suits with squared-off shoulders, wide velvet lapels and cuffs, and thin, straight pants. He rarely had money. He "would stalk the college with a guitar strapped to his back, ready for the lunchtime sessions over scallops and chips . . . with two other kids from the more academic Liverpool Institute next door. Their names were Paul McCartney and George Harrison" (Coleman, p. 71).

In May 1957, Lennon had formed the Quarry Men skiffle group (using instruments such as washboards and combs) with school friends. Paul McCartney had attended a Quarry Men performance at Woolton Parish Church Fete and met John there. He later joined the group.

On July 15, 1958, John's mother, Julia, who had remarried, died at the age of forty-four after being hit by a car while leaving Mimi's house. After his mother's death and the equally untimely death of Buddy Holly, Lennon changed. He continued to study art, but his number one love—music—burst through every layer of his life. At school he campaigned hard, and the student body voted him into the students' union. His personal reason for being voted in was to play rock music.

After he met Paul McCartney, who became his songwriting soul-mate, the two worked with furious and singular enthusiasm developing musical techniques and mastering the guitar. Using the name Nerk Twins (taken from British Air Force slang), they performed successfully. The next year, 1959, they met George Harrison, another guitarist, and Pete Best, the Beatles' future drummer (he was fired in 1962 and replaced by Ringo Starr). The four Quarry Men—John Lennon; Paul McCartney, a brilliant student who came from a musical family; George Harrison, a Liverpool Institute scholar; and Ken Brown, a gifted guitarist—became Johnny and the Moondogs. After this, they became the Moonshiners. Finally, in 1960 the quartet, because of the insistent four-four beat, adopted the name the Silver Beatles. As a quartet, they experimented with banjo sounds accompanied by a washboard. They played in cellar clubs in Liverpool and went on tour with the Larry Parnes Pop Show.

On August 16, 1960, the four Beatles took a tramp steamer to Hamburg, Germany, where they played the red-light district bars of Hamburg seven days a week. They entertained the locals in Hamburg's best-known strip bar known as the Club Indra located on the Reeperbahn, the sordid night-life section of the city. They also played in the Kaiserkeller. They became a quintet when Stuart Sutcliffe, a bass guitarist, joined them; but Sutcliffe didn't play with them long because he died young of a brain tumor (Goldman, p. 136).

On June 2, 1960, the group changed names again and became the Beatles for their first local professional appearance. Ironically, "It was Stu Sutcliffe who suggested that the group call themselves the Beetles. John, who liked to pun with words, changed this to the Beatles" (Leigh, p. 10). At first, the Beatles played for as long as seven hours at each performance. In Hamburg, because they worked so long on stage, they developed their famous and effective technique for ad-libbing and enjoying themselves with the audience. After becoming popular in Hamburg, they worked for several months in the

Cavern, a jazz/beat cellar club in Liverpool city center, close to the Mersey River. In Germany, John bought his first Rickenbacker guitar.

The Beatles returned to Liverpool on December 5, 1960. George Harrison, age seventeen at the time, was deported to England after being arrested and jailed for working in a foreign country while underage. Paul McCartney and Pete Best were ordered to leave Germany after allegedly setting fire to some sacks with a candle behind the cinema screen in the club where they lived. Lennon made his way home alone and penniless.

Recognition of Lennon's genius occurred in October 1961. Brian Epstein, who managed the record and radio department of his family's furniture business, watched the Beatles perform at the Cavern. One day he received a request for the record album *My Bonnie*, recorded by the Beatles as accompaniment for singer Tony Sheridan. Responding to an intuition, Epstein ordered two hundred copies of the record. He felt no surprise when every copy sold within days.

In 1961, Lennon and the Beatles looked typically disheveled, as was the style in the 1960s. The group's main attractions were the words to Lennon's songs, the musicians' uncommon chord combinations, and their personalities. Epstein became the Beatles' manager in January 1962. Also in 1962, on August 23, John Lennon married Cynthia Powell, whom he had met at the Liverpool College of Art. That same evening the Beatles, with Lennon, played in Chester. The very next month, the group recorded their first astonishing single, "Love Me Do."

Epstein changed their appearance by having neat, Edwardian-style collarless suits made for them by haute couture fashion designer Pierre Cardin. Next, he had their hair styled, every head the same. Now they looked neat and proper in a charming medieval, ancient British style. Meanwhile, on April 8, 1963, John and Cynthia's son, John Charles Julian, was born.

> ♪
> **John Lennon**
>
> **Born:**
> October 9, 1940
> Liverpool, England
> **Died:**
> December 8, 1980
> New York City
> **First Hit Single:**
> (with the Beatles)
> "Love Me Do," 1962

Epstein took the Beatles to the United States in 1964. He had booked the group on *The Ed Sullivan Show*, broadcast over CBS-TV. Sullivan's musical director predicted they would not last a year.

The Beatles also appeared in two successful Carnegie Hall concerts. After that, Epstein booked them for visits to Miami and Washington, D.C. Somewhere along the road to their success, Epstein decided the Beatles would become a household word in the United States. With that goal in mind he persuaded Capitol Records, EMI's American subsidiary, to hold a $50,000 publicity campaign to spread the Beatles' name. Their Capitol recording "I Want to Hold Your Hand," written by Lennon and McCartney, became the number one hit before their arrival in the United States and eventually sold more than four million copies. In fact, by the time John Lennon arrived in New York on February 7, 1964, Beatlemania had reached hysterical proportions from one end of the United States to the other.

The Beatles visited twenty-four cities in Canada and the United States. By the time Lennon reached his twenty-fifth birthday in October 1965, the group had embarked on a third U.S. tour. Their fans filled Shea Stadium (fifty-five thousand) in New York City, with tens of thousands of others having been turned away. Later, the Beatles' presence nearly caused a riot at San Francisco's Cow Palace. Later still, on July 5, 1966, on tour in the South Pacific, after the Beatles were accused of snubbing the president's wife, riots broke out in Manila, the capital of the Philippines.

On November 9, 1966, John Lennon met Japanese artist Yoko Ono while she exhibited her work in London at the Indica Gallery. One of her pieces was an apple, with a price that was close to four hundred dollars. Lennon called the price absurd, saying he didn't have to pay all that money for an apple. After this, Yoko asked John to climb a stepladder and hammer an imaginary nail into the wall.

When John met Yoko, he lived in the cyclonic fury of Beatlemania. Never fulfilled by fame and money, he was ready for a new force in his life. At the same time, never one to rush, his flirtation with Yoko took months.

In 1967, the Beatles and their wives went by train from London to attend a seminar on meditation by the Maharishi Mahesh Yogi. At the station John's wife, Cynthia, missed the train by seconds. Lennon disappeared onto the train without her. Also in 1967, Brian Epstein, after steering the Beatles to the dizziest heights known to world fame, died on August 27 of an accidental drug overdose.

Early in 1968 John and Cynthia traveled to Rishikesh, India with George and Patti Harrison to attend the Maharishi's meditation academy. Lennon became a serious pupil of meditation (which was seeing a resurgence in the 1960s as one way to escape the speed and aggravations of everyday life). He sometimes meditated eight hours a day during the eight weeks he spent at the academy, which resulted in fifteen new songs.

In the meantime, John continued seeing Yoko. In August 1968, Cynthia sued John for divorce on the grounds of adultery with Yoko Ono. In October, John and Yoko announced that they were expecting a baby in February 1969; but Yoko had a miscarriage. In 1969, Yoko Ono divorced Anthony Cox, and on March 20, 1969, John and Yoko flew from Paris to Gibraltar, where they remained for just over an hour, long enough to be married. During the summer of 1969, when Lennon was twenty-nine years old and suddenly immensely wealthy and successful, his father tried to reenter his life, but Lennon did not renew the relationship. "John told friends that he would have preferred to have totally resolved his relationship with his father but that obviously it was not possible" (Coleman, p. 512).

In 1970, the Beatles, which had formed in the late 1950s, disbanded amid infighting, feeling they had exhausted their possibilities as a group. The members at this time were John Lennon, Paul McCartney, George Harrison, and Ringo Starr (Richard Starkey).

Clever with words, Lennon had written many of the songs that brought the Beatles fame. His lyrics were the opposite of those of most American rock 'n' roll singers. Lennon's songs had a playful, positive, lighthearted approach to love. He never expressed emotions such as jealousy and hate. Even his song titles display a playful attitude; "And I Love Her," "All My Loving," and "I Saw Her Standing There."

John and Yoko separated in 1973 after four and a half years of marriage and reunited in January 1975. After the reunion Yoko became pregnant, and at age forty-two she gave birth at a New York hospital to the couple's first child—a son, Sean Taro Ono Lennon.

Writing since his teens, Lennon completed two successful books of prose and verse. He illustrated both with his own sketches, and both became overnight best-sellers. Lennon's second book topped the first. The toughest critics found influences from English writer and mathematician Lewis Carroll (1832–1898), American humorous writer and cartoonist James Thurber (1894–1961), and Irish novelist James Joyce (1882–1941).

On December 8, 1980 (December 9 in the United Kingdom), John Lennon was shot in the back and killed by former hospital security guard Mark David Chapman, age twenty-five, who, clutching a copy of John and Yoko's *Double Fantasy* album, had gotten John's autograph six hours earlier. On December 10, Lennon was cremated in New York State.

> John Lennon was not only a genius. He was also a man of profound commitment, total integrity, and intensive activity: a glance at the sheer volume and pattern of his life's work confirms that. His honesty and wit, his vulnerability, his lack of

---

♪

Interesting Facts about John Lennon

At art school in Liverpool, he campaigned to become a member of the student union so he could play rock music at school.

Starting out with the Beatles, he played for as long as seven hours at each performance.

He wrote two books of prose and verse, illustrating both with his own sketches; both became overnight best-sellers.

---

pomposity, his unique artistry, spirit, and romanticism endeared him to millions. The grief that followed his murder, and the celebrations of his life and work, spanned the world. As a twentieth-century philosopher, he set an example of imagination and humanitarianism. Although he would hate to be deified, a light went out on 8 December 1980. But his music and his spirit shine on. (Coleman, p. 691)

Bibliography

Coleman, Ray. *Lennon: The Definitive Biography*. New York: Harper-Perennial, 1992.

Conord, Bruce W. *John Lennon*. Broomall, Pa.: Chelsea House, 1993.

Goldman, Albert. *The Lives of John Lennon*. New York: Bantam Books, 1989.

Leigh, Vanora. *John Lennon*. New York: Bookwright Press, 1986.

Midori

(1971–)

Critics cite Midori, a spectacular Japanese-born prodigy, as the most distinguished violinist of the latter part of the twentieth century. Midori began playing the violin at age four. At age six, her public career began. In 1981, at age ten, she reduced renowned violinist Pinchas Zukerman to tears when she played Bartók's Second Violin Concerto. At age eleven, a standing ovation sealed her debut with the New York Philharmonic. The White House witnessed her mastery before she was a teenager. Worldwide fame caught her by the time she reached age fourteen in 1986.

Midori was born in Osaka, Japan, on October 25, 1971. Her father was a successful engineer. Her mother, Setsu Goto, a professional violinist, said she felt her baby's sensitivity to music almost from the moment the child was born. When only two years old Midori slept on a front seat in the audience of the auditorium when her mother rehearsed.

It is interesting to note that her name wasn't originally Midori. Midori Goto changed her name to Mi Dori in 1983, the year her parents divorced. Later, she decided on the single word *Midori*.

Midori's career began in a simple way. One day her mother heard her humming a Bach concerto, the exact piece she had practiced a few days before. Following this, fascinated by her mother's violin, the child climbed onto the piano bench trying to reach the violin kept on top of the family piano. When Midori reached her third birthday, Setsu encouraged her young daughter's budding interest in music by giving her a tiny, 1/16th-size violin. Following the birthday gift, Setsu began teaching her three-year-old the violin.

At age six, Midori performed before an audience for the first time. She played a caprice by the nineteenth-century Italian violinist Niccolò Paganini (1782–1840), who had made his own debut at age eleven in 1793. With no admonishments from her mother or reminders from anyone, the young girl practiced daily. Long hours with the violin every day trained her in a way nothing else could, and her progress kept a steady pace.

As she grew older, Midori accompanied her mother to concert halls where Setsu rehearsed by the hour for upcoming performances. While her mother played onstage with the orchestra, Midori practiced alone in a nearby empty room.

Midori

AP/Wide World Photos

When Midori was eight years old, an American colleague, a friend of her mother, accidentally heard Midori play the violin. Overwhelmed by the child's precocious ease of technical facility, unimaginable under those tiny fingers, she took a tape recording of Midori's music to Dorothy DeLay, the renowned violin instructor at New York City's Juilliard School of Music. So extraordinarily did Midori's music shine through the homemade tape that even the poor sound quality did not detract from its effect. DeLay, accustomed to hearing violin prodigies, was astonished by Midori's extraordinary performances of difficult works by Paganini, Bach, and French composer Camille Saint-Saëns (1835–1921). In 1981, DeLay accepted Midori as a scholarship student at the Aspen, Colorado, Music Festival. Playing the chaconne from Bach's Violin Partita no. 2 in D Minor like a seasoned veteran of countless performances, Midori made her U.S. debut in Aspen.

Midori's phenomenal performance of the difficult piece confirmed DeLay's initial evaluation of the nine-year-old as one of the most remarkable violin prodigies she had ever witnessed. The performance prompted an invitation from violinist Pinchas Zukerman, who asked the child to perform before his master class at Aspen. She played a Bartók concerto.

> "Out comes this tiny little thing, not even ten at the time," Zukerman later told the critic K. Robert Schwartz. "I was sitting on a chair and I was tall as she was standing. She turned, she bowed to the audience, she bowed to me, she bowed to the pianist. . . . She had a tiny little half-size violin, but the sound that came out—it was ridiculous. I was absolutely stunned. I turned to the audience and said, Ladies and gentlemen, I don't know about you, but I've just witnessed a miracle." (Page, p. 12)

In 1982, when Midori was eleven years old, her mother gave up her own performing career in Japan to move with her daughter to New York City. Midori enrolled on a full scholarship at Juilliard in the pre-college division. After this, her parents divorced and Midori and her mother began a new life together in America.

Midori so impressed Zubin Mehta, the music director of the New York Philharmonic, during her first year of study at Juilliard that he featured her as a surprise guest soloist in the Philharmonic's traditional New Year's Eve concert. She overwhelmed the audience and received a standing ovation.

♪
Midori
Born:
October 25, 1971
Osaka, Japan
First CD:
Paganini: 24 Caprices, 1989

Simultaneously, Midori attended school and studied hard. She took music classes at Juilliard and attended the Professional Children's School for academic subjects. In this way, she continued her education with a full academic schedule. At the same time, she continued to perform with the New York Philharmonic for young people's galas and concerts. On one program, which she considers one of the happiest moments of her life, she played a movement from Vivaldi's Concerto for Three Violins with two of her favorite performers, Isaac Stern and Pinchas Zukerman.

An especially important appearance at this time included a performance for President and Mrs. Reagan. The concert, televised, became a part of the White House Christmas program in Washington, D.C.

Despite increasing public demand to hear her performances, Midori's manager, Lee Lamont of ICM Artists, limited her concert appearances. This gave her time to polish and broaden an already impressive repertoire. One might think she could coast for a while. But she pushed herself at every turn. Dorothy DeLay, at Juilliard, said that at age ten Midori was capable of managing more of the usual repertoire than most violinists twice her age.

In May 1985, at age fourteen, Midori made her Canadian debut performing Mendelssohn's Violin Concerto with the Toronto Symphony conducted by Pinchas Zukerman. Two months later, she traveled to Japan to perform with Leonard Bernstein and the European Youth Orchestra in a distinctive concert marking the fortieth anniversary of the bombing of Hiroshima. Not long after returning to the United States, Midori left for a national tour. She appeared as a guest soloist with a number of regional symphony orchestras and, later, at several summer music festivals.

She still studied with Dorothy DeLay at Juilliard in New York. However, in 1987 she terminated all instruction with her famous teacher. Midori insists this was her first adult decision. She says her mother asked her to go back for one more lesson, but she didn't.

By the time DeLay no longer taught Midori violin in 1987, Midori had already reached the status of a recognized celebrity. She had made her reputation the summer before at the Tanglewood Music Festival in Massachusetts.

Midori appeared as guest soloist with the Boston Symphony Orchestra, the festival's resident orchestra, under the baton of Leonard Bernstein. Her unprecedented professional manners under the most inconceivable pressure gained her near-legendary fame among classical music enthusiasts. In fact, her commanding performance launched her to the front page of the *New York Times*.

During the long and strenuous fifth and final movement of Bernstein's Serenade for Violin and String Orchestra, under the composer's direction, the E-string on Midori's violin, a slightly smaller than normal Guarnerius del Gesu, broke. Without faltering, she took up the concertmaster's Stradivarius (a much larger instrument than her own), strapped on her own chin rest, and continued the fifth movement. Then the seemingly impossible happened. The E-string on the Stradivarius snapped. Again, without hesitating, with no visible signs of anxiety, she borrowed the associate concertmaster's Guadagnini, attached her chin rest to this violin during a break in the music, and completed the serenade and the performance in perfect tranquility.

The orchestra members, the audience, and Bernstein himself exploded in applause. Audience, orchestra, and conductor-composer honored her with a thunderous cheering, stamping, whistling ovation. The next day, the expected photograph and story on the front page of the *New York Times* shocked no one. Genuinely bewildered by the appreciation and acclaim her performance brought her, she let it be known that she had continued to play because she didn't want to stop.

She loved Bernstein's Serenade and, no matter what happened, was determined to finish it.

Midori's performance at Tanglewood was a turning point in her career. She received instant fame in the media and the highest possible praise from music critics. Acclaimed by scholars, critics, and every imaginable other professional, she is recognized today as an astonishingly, accomplished master technician.

During the summer of 1987, Midori returned to Tanglewood and Aspen. She also added four new destinations to her itinerary. At the Hollywood Bowl Summer Festival, the Montreal Symphony featured her as soloist. At the Blossom Music Festival in Ohio, she appeared with the Cleveland Orchestra. At the Ravinia Festival in suburban Chicago, she was in performance with the St. Paul Chamber Orchestra; and finally, she performed in the Mostly Mozart Festival at Lincoln Center for the Performing Arts in New York City.

Midori has appeared as a guest soloist with many of the world's most important orchestras. They include the Berlin Philharmonic, the Philadelphia Orchestra, l'Orchestre de Paris, the Los Angeles Philharmonic, the Vienna symphony, and the Monte Carlo Philharmonic. She toured the United States in 1988 with the Monte Carlo Philharmonic in a program featuring Polish violinist and composer Henryk Wieniawski's (1835–1880) Violin Concerto in F-sharp Minor. She made her official New York orchestral debut in May 1989 with a weeklong appearance in a New York Philharmonic subscription program at Avery Fisher Hall, playing Dvořák's Concerto in A Minor.

On her personal stage, Midori attends concerts, goes to movies, and enjoys writing short stories, reading, and studying karate. She has contributed to a column in a Japanese teen magazine on life in the United States. Also, she gives time to "Midori and Friends," a foundation she established to bring working musicians to teach and perform for children in the classrooms of New York public schools. She established the foundation in 1992. Since then it has expanded from a one-person operation to an organization with a full-time staff, corporate sponsors, and an annual budget of $500,000. In 1997, "Midori and Friends"

♪
Interesting Facts about Midori

When she was a child she played a concert for President Reagan and his wife, Nancy, which became part of the White House Christmas program in Washington, D.C.

During her first performance at Tanglewood in Massachusetts at the age of fourteen, her own violin broke, but she finished the piece anyway with first another violin that broke a string and then a third violin. This performance brought her instant fame and praise from music critics.

She has contributed to a column in a Japanese teen magazine on life in the United States.

sponsored 125 events in 22 schools. The foundation's purpose is to show children that involvement in music does not have to be aimed in the direction of a career, that music can bring delight and pleasure to them throughout their lives.

Although she has cut back a hectic schedule that at one time included ninety-five concerts annually, Midori estimates she spends only seven or eight weeks a year at home. The rest of the time she travels. New England, Mexico, and Israel she has named as her favorite places.

Midori has also gone into the recording industry. She has released double concertos of German organist Johann Sebastian Bach (1685–1750) and noted Italian violinist and composer Antonio Vivaldi (1678–1741) with Pinchas Zuckerman (1948–). She has also released two violin concertos by Hungarian composer Béla Bartók (1881–1945), the violin concerto of Czechoslovakian Antonin Dvorák (1841–1904), and caprices by Italian composer Niccolò Paganini (1782–1840). Her contract with CBS Masterworks is exclusive. She makes her own selections for recordings and chooses the orchestra and conductor for accompaniment.

During her career, Midori has received numerous awards. The Japanese government cited her as Best Artist of the Year in 1988. She is the youngest person ever to receive this award. She accepted the Dorothy B. Chandler Performing Arts Award in September 1989 from the Los Angeles Music Center. She was also given the Crystal Award from the *Asahi Shimbun*, Japan's most widely read newspaper, for her promotion of the arts.

Bibliography

Charnan, Simon. *Midori: Brilliant Violinist*. Danbury, Conn.: Children's Press, 1993.

Detroit Free Press, February 5, 1995.

"Midori 1971– ." U.X.L. Biographies, Online. Subscribed-to program, June 20, 2000. 1999.

Page, Tim. "Caught Between Snoopy and her Stradivarius . . . Midori at 21." *Newsday*, September 19, 1993, p. 12.

♪

Wolfgang Amadeus Mozart

(1756–1791)

Mozart, an eighteenth-century Austrian composer with gifts of extraordinary genius, was one of the most perfectly talented and creative musicians the world has ever known. Only two names, Wolfgang Amadeus Mozart and Joseph Haydn (1732–1809), stand at the helm of the classical style in the late eighteenth century. "In natural gifts [Mozart] was one of the most perfectly equipped musicians who ever lived" (Scholes, p. 662).

Mozart composed and performed with technical perfection on the harpsichord, violin, and piano. Beginning his musical career as a mere infant, by the time he was four years old he composed music. Furthermore, throughout his early childhood years he never stopped creating, rewriting, perfecting. By the age of seven, he astonished individuals from the highest royalty to the lowest peasant with performances unequaled in any part of civilization where music could be enjoyed.

Born in Salzburg, Austria, in 1756, Mozart began life in brilliant sun and ended under dark clouds. By age ten the child, destined to live a life of grim poverty, had toured Europe as a prodigy. Until his early death in Vienna (at the time one of the music capitals of Europe) on December 5, 1791, at the age of thirty-five, he performed at the keyboard, played the organ in churches, and conducted operas he had written. During his short life he composed with ease and without cease; ideas and notes flowed so profusely from an inner fountain that he completed more than six hundred musical works.

Indeed, Mozart composed some of the most magnificent works of classical music known to the world, including piano concertos, symphonies, operas, and string quartets. Although he could not make a living with it, he spent his entire life obsessed with music. At age seven, his ear was so keen and exact and his musical memory so powerful that he could detect a difference of a mere eighth of a tone and recall it without error the following day.

Friends told a story that he had played the violin of a musician friend named Schachtner, his favorite because of its soft, smooth tone—so lovely, in fact, that he nicknamed it the butter fiddle. One day, however, Schachtner found the young child amusing himself with his own little violin. The butter fiddle was nowhere around, and Mozart wondered what had happened to it. He told Schachtner that if the tuning of the violin had not been altered since he last played it, it was a half a quarter of a tone flatter than that of the little violin he held. Schachtner laughed at this stupendous exactitude of ear and memory in a mere child. But Mozart's father, understanding his son's gift, had the violin examined. Mozart was correct. The violin played a half a quarter of a tone flatter than his own little violin.

Wolfgang Amadeus Mozart

In the circle of professional musicians within which the Mozart family lived, everyone agreed that the seven-year-old child had a one-in-a-million absolute pitch ear capable of detecting the most minute and the nearly immeasurable differences beyond a half a quarter of a tone. Yet even as Mozart's miraculous talents matured and attracted the attention of the most cultivated and wealthiest patrons of the arts, including royalty, he never found professional success. So far above the works of the best composers were his compositions that only a few knowledgeable musicians understood and fully appreciated his music.

Moreover, his music was resented and disparaged by fellow composers of far lesser ability.

Apart from Mozart's music's emotional associations and significance, it is flawless in melodic shape, in rhythmic interest, in natural yet original harmonic coloring, and (if orchestral) in the provocative yet dignified form of its instrumental treatment. Only after Mozart died did a few individuals acknowledge his contributions to music. It is said that he never stopped thinking about music. The ceaseless, ever-flowing rhythms in his mind may have been what caused him to always tap his watch fob, a table, a chair-back, or anything at hand. Surprisingly, he played billiards. Some historians think he loved these ball games not for the sake of the game but because he found in the movement and control of a rolling ball the ideal accompaniment to the unceasing churning within his mind.

Instances are recorded of his stopping in the middle of a game to write musical notations, or of his humming, as he played the game, a theme that some people recognized later in his compositions. He preferred playing billiards alone, with his notebook within reach, although the notes he made were only brief indications of an idea. Mozart did his actual composing in his head. His father had taught him well.

"Leopold Mozart, himself a gifted and cultured musician (of some European reputation as the author of a violin 'school'), was an intelligent teacher and a wise parent, and gave [his son] that firm foundation of sound musical and general instruction which his natural endowment deserved" (Scholes, p. 663). Leopold recognized early that his small son had a rare talent. In fact, he referred to his son as a God-given miracle and began the boy's music lessons early. "Leopold lost no time in teaching his children music and in 1760 he made a note alongside the first eight pieces in Nannerl's [Mozart's sister] music book that 'the preceding 8 minuets were learnt by Wolfgangerl in his 4th year'" (Baker, p. 16).

By age three, the child could play chords on the keyboard. By age four, he began learning composition, harpsichord, and violin. Perhaps most remarkable, the boy showed an ability to play a melody with incredible and complete exactness after hearing it only one time.

After Mozart's death, his sister, four years older, Marianne von Berchtold (always called Nannerl), authenticated details of their shared childhood. Mozart was the seventh child of a family in which only two survived, and his birth nearly killed his mother, Maria Anna Pertl. After Leopold started Nannerl on the harpsichord when she was seven years old, little Wolfgang, who was about three, played at the keyboard using Nannerl's *Notenbuch*, or music book. In its margins Leopold scribbled sentences that stand as evidence of his son's genius, his ability to perform competently and exactly at three years of age.

Leopold included details in a few of his notes. Alongside one particular composition Leopold wrote that Wolfgang, when four years old, learned a minuet; and the child's first compositions, two keyboard pieces, appeared in Nannerl's *Notenbuch*. Both are written in his father's hand. At age five, Mozart composed minuets, all classics that first-year piano students practice today. When the boy reached six years of age, he went to the court in Vienna and played for the Austrian empress. Before he reached his seventh birthday, he composed eight more compositions.

Under their father's guidance, Mozart and his older sister visited cities in Germany, England, and France. During the tour, Mozart's acclaim as a prodigy turned to personal power for Leopold, and he soon justified his entire existence with his new, self-appointed position of authority. At the same time, the small child's most important reward was his father's approval. Thus he reacted with rapid and faithful obedience to all of Leopold's concerns. His young life became a structured existence.

Nannerl recalled a ritual conducted every night at bedtime until Mozart reached the age of ten. The child sang any melody he made up on the spot, and Leopold sang expertly in counterpoint. Once the two finished their "song," Mozart kissed his father and fell asleep. "Next to God comes Papa" became his childhood motto. "It is clear that Mozart loved his parents, and particularly his father, very dearly" (Baker, p. 25).

In London in the spring of 1764, Mozart was eight years old. Scientist Daines Barrington studied and tested his uncanny genius to improvise vocal works for various effects such as love, rage, and anger in all types of songs. After telling the boy he would like to hear a spontaneous love song such as one might select for an opera, the examination began. According to Barrington, even before the test ended he knew nothing could improve the music the eight-year-old composed.

Barrington said Mozart sat at the harpsichord watching him with childish cunning. Then he played four or five lines of a solo suitable as a prelude to a love song. He followed this bit of lighthearted flourish with a composition that might complement a melody composed for *Affetto* (affection). When Barrington discovered that the boy had become enthused he requested a song of rage, one that might be appropriate for an opera. The child again looked around shrewdly and played six or seven masterful lines. His notes seemed the perfect beginning to a song meant to indicate anger. During the exercise the child became so angry that he beat the harpsichord with his fist, rose from his chair, and fell back again.

The eight-year-old also impressed the eminent historian Charles Burney. During a performance, Mozart revealed an incredible knowledge of vocalizing, imitating the unique styles of several opera singers as well as their songs in an opera he invented on the spot using nonsense words. At the end, he added an overture in two movements, all improvised with taste and imagination, correct harmony, melody, and modulation. After this performance, he played marbles like a child.

During the London season, where the allure of money attracted him, Leopold wrote enthusiastically that he had finally found a way to make enough money so that his family could be comfortable for life. When their London residence neared its end, Leopold had his two prodigies on public view every day and hoped for enormous profits.

Unfortunately, the usual format of Mozart's public performances was nothing more than a common stage show where audiences expected ordinary songs, dances, skits, theatrical comic pieces, and acrobatic performances. At some point within all this, someone would announce to the audience that a prodigy would masterfully play a concerto on the violin and accompany symphonies on the clavier (the generic term for the stringed keyboard instruments). Then Mozart would accurately name from a distance any notes that were sounded for him in chords on the clavier. Last, he would improvise, not only on the organ but also on the pianoforte.

Mozart's father, ever the tireless manager, took advantage of his son's stunning successes. Furthermore, no one objected. In fact, men, women, and children clamored at every appearance to hear the small boy play more. At a local tavern, anyone could pay two shillings and six pence to hear him.

In his efforts to get his children before audiences as frequently as possible and in as many places for as much money as possible, Leopold risked his children's health. Yet no one is able to judge whether Mozart and his sister would have been safer at home in Salzburg, where germs of unchecked epidemics and foreign diseases entered the city daily. Indeed, safety and cure from viruses and bacteria did not exist. Given the fact that Mozart fell critically ill and even came close to dying six or eight times during his childhood travels, one can only be amazed that his output did not suffer. In Paris and London, he lay near death with rheumatic fever and acute tonsillitis. In Paris, his fever stayed abnormally high. In The Hague, he suffered with typhoid fever. In Munich, he again wrestled with rheumatic fever, the sickness that taunted him throughout his life.

> ♪
> **Wolfgang Amadeus Mozart**
>
> **Born:**
> January 27, 1756
> Salzburg, Austria
> **Died:**
> December 5, 1791
> Vienna, Austria
> **Number of Works Composed:**
> Over 600

Nevertheless, after returning home to Salzburg, only nine months passed before Leopold took the child and his sister on the road again. He set out in September 1767 with the entire family for Vienna. Mozart was eleven years old at the time. Especially significant is the fact that in Vienna a smallpox epidemic raged, and of course both children caught the disease. In late October, the Mozarts went to Olmütz in Bohemia, but there was no escape. Delirious with the disease, Mozart was taken to the Cathedral Deanery, where his long convalescence began. Nearly four months had elapsed since the Mozarts had left Salzburg, the major concern then being not smallpox but hope for an audience with Emperor Joseph II.

Finally, ten days after they returned to Vienna from Bohemia, Emperor Joseph II received Mozart. During this time Mozart, in good health, gave musical impromptus at the keyboard before the king and queen. Johann Christian Bach (1732–1795), the eighteenth child of the famous Johann Sebastian, accompanied him.

In a letter to Salzburg, Leopold wrote that the emperor twice asked his son if he would not only compose an opera but agree to conduct it himself. The child, only twelve years old and probably guided by his father, said such a project would bring him true happiness. Ultimately, though, the tide of easily gained good fortune turned. Leopold suspected that plotting by Vienna's best, although jealous, composers had incensed the lead singers and turned everyone against his son in order to prevent the performance of Mozart's opera.

Thinking only of the family's financial situation, Leopold wrote the emperor Joseph II a letter of complaint. He accused the theater's maestro of preventing the performance, and he demanded unpaid performance fees and an expense reimbursement. Although the family returned home with guaranteed satisfaction, Mozart's comic Italian-style opera *La finta semplice* (The Pretended Simpleton) never played to an audience in Vienna.

The twelve-year-old boy, who had never visited Italy, showed an uncanny knowledge of the Italian language in his opera. He also revealed his easy manipulation of languages, delighting in verbally mischievous sentences. On the storming chaos of words and music in his mind, he imposed a quiet, mature, perfect order. He wrote superbly structured arias and ensemble finales supported by orchestral accompaniments that far outdistanced the mediocre achievements of the jealous, contemporary opera composers.

In December 1769, Leopold and Mozart, now age thirteen, headed south to Italy. The trip included forty stops, where Mozart performed in his usual way. During his first visit to Milan, Mozart obtained his first Italian commission from the governor-general of Lombardy, Count Carlo di Firmian, who asked him to write one of his favorite stories from Roman history as an opera. Then the count scheduled a performance for the next carnival season in Milan's Teatro Regio Ducale. They agreed on one hundred ducats by contract in order to avoid another financial crisis such as the one Leopold had faced in Vienna.

Therefore, after receiving Count Firmian's commission, the Mozarts left Milan and stayed in Rome for a month. On Easter Sunday, Pope Clement XIV received father and son. At this time, only fourteen years old, Mozart accepted knighthood. The Pope further insisted that the Order of the Golden Spur be conferred on the boy who had excelled in music since early childhood. With the knighthood secured, father and son continued traveling throughout southern Italy for the next three months. As a result of Mozart's knighthood, his father requested him to sign his compositions "Cavaliere Amadeo."

On their return to Bologna in mid-July, Mozart received the text for his new opera, a text (libretto) based on Jean Racine's *Mithridate*. The ancient play had been staged in Paris one hundred years earlier. Over a four-month period, the Italian writer Vittorio Cigna-Santi had turned his translation of Racine's tragedy into a dramatic new opera text. After thorough study of the new text, Mozart composed the recitatives (the prose and dialogue of an opera). He spent only five months writing his first Italian opera; and because the singers received their assigned roles later, he composed the solos after he became acquainted with the singers and knew their voices. Mozart's entire score contains an opening or overture and twenty-five numbers. Not one of his other operas has so many versions, brief instrumental compositions, fragments, and complex versions of every section.

Less than two weeks before the first scheduled performance, several jealous plots against Mozart became evident. Rumors circulated that it would be impossible for a young Austrian boy to compose an Italian opera. But after the first orchestral rehearsal, the child's remarkable performance ended all mudslinging.

After the grand tour, Mozart stayed at home in Salzburg for several months. At this time he moved toward a career in the theater, a pursuit he followed until he died. When only eleven years old, he successfully transformed such diverse and complex material as a biblical text, a Latin school play, and a parody on a work by Rousseau. He also composed scores of music, set them in musical notation for an orchestra and singers, and conducted the performances from the harpsichord in the late-eighteenth-century tradition.

The Mozart children also continued to perform. They played in concert at the court of the Empress Maria Theresa in Vienna. They performed in the noble households of London, Paris, and central Europe. All the while, Mozart's development as a composer was stupefying. In his first thirteen years he had composed symphonies, sonatas, concertos, and the German operetta *Bastien und Bastienne*. While on tour

> ♪
> **Interesting Facts about Wolfgang Amadeus Mozart**
>
> He began composing music at the age of four.
>
> He would stop in the middle of playing games in order to write musical notations of compositions that came into his mind while playing.
>
> He never found professional success during his lifetime.

in Italy for the three years between 1768 and 1771, he seriously studied the Italian style and received ovations for his concerts in Rome and other major cities. He also successfully produced the opera *Mitridate, re di Ponto* in 1770 at the age of fourteen.

Mozart's tenure at Salzburg occurred during the 1770s. He focused on performing and composing to fulfill his court duties, and at the same time composed for friends and patrons.

When Archbishop Schrattenbach died on December 16, 1771, Hieronymus Colloredo became the new archbishop in March 1772. He changed the archdiocese that once favored cultural life and attracted prominent writers and scientists. Significant to Mozart's life was the archbishop's decision to eliminate court music. Archbishop Colloredo closed the university theater in 1778 and shortened the Mass at church. He placed restriction on the performance of purely instrumental music.

Undaunted, Mozart composed enthusiastically during the early years of Colloredo's rule, especially between 1772 and 1774, while still in his teens. After 1774, however, he began to withdraw from Salzburg court music. (The reasons for his dissatisfaction are unknown.) After this, Leopold could not find suitable positions for either of them. The lack of work was compounded by constant troubles with Archbishop Colloredo.

On August 21, 1772 Mozart became the court Konzertmeister (concert master, leader of the first violin section of a symphony orchestra who plays the solo passages and may serve as assistant to the conductor), a position he held for nearly three years. Leopold continued to supervise court music, responsible for securing musicians, music, and instruments. Yet father and son remained unhappy in Salzburg, and the archbishop's ultimate rejection of them may have been for reasons other than their employment. Speculation turns to Colloredo's personality, his music reforms in Salzburg, and the changes he made concerning court music.

Mozart then turned away from court life. He tended to his duties and composed church music, but with little enthusiasm. The situation culminated in the summer of 1777 when Mozart asked the archbishop for his release from employment. Colloredo dismissed both father and son.

With his mother, Mozart traveled again and visited European cities, including Munich and Mannheim, where he fell briefly in love with the singer Aloysia Webber. He also traveled to Paris. Despite the successful Paris performance of his Symphony in D (1778), known as the *Paris* Symphony, Mozart did not receive full French approbation. Still, seldom disheartened, he continued to write.

When Mozart's mother died while he and Leopold were in Salzburg, his father, feeling helpless, blamed Mozart for laziness, lying, and neglect of his mother. When a post opened as court organist in 1778, Archbishop Colloredo reinstated him. At first he worked diligently, but his compositions did not satisfy Colloredo who expected the musician to take a larger role in court music. During his final years in Salzburg, Mozart appeared as both performer and composer, but he preferred composing for private friends and the local nobility.

He traveled to Munich, Germany in 1780 to fulfill a commission for the opera *Idomeneo* (1781) for the Bavarian court. The performers loved him, but the opera did not further his career. After this, Colloredo directed him to Vienna where the archbishop was living with his court temporarily. Happy after his success in Munich, Mozart was offended in Vienna at being treated so poorly, and the letters he wrote home over the next three months revealed his resentment. Among other insults, the archbishop curtailed his performances. On May 9, 1781, matters exploded during Mozart's interview with Colloredo when the musician requested his discharge. At first, the archbishop refused him, but finally released him, again, from Salzburg service.

Before Mozart had left Italy in 1773, he wrote *Exsultate, Jubilate*, a motet (an unaccompanied polyphonic sacred song). He wrote *Exsultate, Jubilate* especially for the castrato soprano (artificial male soprano) Venanzio Rauzzini (1746–1810) who first sang the new motet with the orchestra in Milan's Theotine Church. Mozart was not yet seventeen years old.

In the final movement of this work, now identified as K. 165, Mozart treats the word *Alleluia* in a way that requires breathtaking virtuosity from the singer, technical skill and accomplishment beyond that expected of a pianist or violinist performing his instrumental concertos. As Mozart expected, Rauzzini made not a single mistake.

Mozart married when he was twenty-six years old and lived in poverty with rare periods of public success. His sister, Nannerl, wrote "that he married a girl quite unsuited to him, and this led to the great domestic chaos at and after his death" (Baker, p. 26). During his later years, he began his series of great operas. He wrote *The Marriage of Figaro* in his thirtieth year and *Don Giovanni* in his thirty-second.

Also at age thirty-two (1788), he composed the three symphonies that rank as not only his greatest but among the greatest the world has ever heard. He wrote one in E flat, one in G minor, and one in C, today called *Jupiter*. Mozart belonged to the Order of Freemasons and wrote several compositions for their meetings. Masonic traditions and beliefs inspired the fairy-tale opera *The Magic Flute* in his thirty-fifth year. It is still popular today.

During his brief career, Mozart wrote nearly fifty symphonies, close to twenty operas and operettas, over twenty piano concertos, twenty-seven string quartets, about forty violin sonatas, and a quantity of other music. His last work was *Requiem*, on which he worked like a man possessed with the foreboding that it would commemorate his own death. He died without finishing *Requiem*; it was left to a pupil to complete.

Mozart probably died from uremia. He was thirty-five years old. Near the end, he asked his wife to keep his death a secret until his friend Albrechtsberger could apply for the job to succeed him in a post that had recently been given him, that of *capellmeister* of the St. Stephen's Cathedral. A very frugal funeral took place in which few friends accompanied the coffin, burial was in the common spot allotted to paupers, and no one marked the grave.

Today, audiences enjoy and appreciate Mozart's works more widely than those of any composer. Mozart's works, written in almost every possible musical variety and type, combine a brilliant beauty of sound with classical elegance and perfect technical accuracy. Of all the instrumental works written in the history of music, his are probably the most articulate. Apart from their emotional significance, his compositions have no equal in melodic shape, rhythmic interest, and natural yet completely innovative harmonic coloring. So perfect were his compositions that many have remained in the modern performance repertoire for more than two hundred years.

Bibliography

Baker, Richard. *Mozart*. New York: Thames and Hudson, 1982.

Robbins Landon, H.C., ed. *The Mozart Compendium: A Guide to Mozart's Life and Music*. New York: Schirmer Books, 1990.

Sadie, Stanley. *The New Grove Mozart*. New York: Norton, 1982.

Scholes, Percy A. *The Oxford Companion to Music*, 10th ed. London: Oxford University Press, 1978.

♪

Niccolò Paganini

(1782–1840)

Violinist Niccolò Paganini, a prodigy, had a virtuosity that became legendary during his brief life of fifty-eight years. Those who heard him play sometimes reacted to his ineffably beautiful melodies by bursting into tears. At other times, he performed with such force and passion that people claimed he had the devil guide his bow. Once he became famous, his life was one of triumphant performance and luxurious living. Yet on one occasion he had to pawn his violin to pay a gambling debt, and a French merchant loaned him a Guarneri violin (second only to Stradivari in the history of violin making) so that he could play a concert. After hearing the performance, the merchant told Paganini he could keep the instrument.

Paganini was born in the poorest circumstances in Genoa, Italy, October 27, 1782, in a three-room dwelling on the seventh story of an old house at 38 Passo di Gattamora, sometimes called Alley of the Black Cat. The ancient house still stands, and an inscription reads: "High venture sprang from this humble place. In this house on 27 October 1782 Niccolò Paganini was born to adorn Genoa and delight the world" (Kenneson, p. 66).

Although greeted by grim poverty when he entered the world, Paganini had an innate genius for the violin. Driven, he worked with the instrument sometimes to the point of near collapse. His unnumbered hours of practice brought him first to high honor and then to grand wealth.

Paganini did more than become expertly accomplished on the violin. He extended the range of the instrument from its lowest to its highest tone by harmonics, a music practice known as *scordatura,* or different, complex tunings of the strings. The stories of his wondrous technical feats gave him a supernatural glamour. In fact, many fans sincerely believed he was a figure from heaven. His violin compositions have formed the basis for piano music by German romantic composer Robert Schumann (1810–1856), Hungarian composer Franz Liszt (1811–1886), German composer Johannes Brahms (1833–1897), and Russian composer Sergei Rachmaninoff (1873–1943).

Not all Paganini's biographers believed the stories one can find about him enough to publish them. A few, however, perpetuated some of the supernatural myths with stories of prophetic visions and dreams his mother, Teresa Bocciardo Paganini, described. Conveyed via Genoese folk culture, his mother's forecasts add a mood of otherworldliness to the mysterious eighteenth-century image of Paganini. An angelic annunciation at the time of his birth is but one of Teresa's fabrications.

In his personal life, Paganini always remained a private person. In fact, he was nearly fifty years old before he told biographers anything concerning his childhood. Conversations with biographers in 1830 produced two autobiographical sketches. Peter Lichtenthal in Leipzig published one, and Julius Schottky in Prague published another. Both believe Paganini did not tell all the details concerning several important events in his life. However, scant revelations and bits and pieces of stories have enabled historians to put together a great deal of what occurred during his early childhood.

© Leonard de Selva/CORBIS

Niccolò Paganini

Peter Lichtenthal's 1830 biographical sketch, *Allgemeine Musikalische,* gives Paganini's birth date as the eve of St. Simeon's Day, 1784. Other accounts say he was born two years earlier, the son of Antonio and Teresa Bocciardo, both amateur musicians. When Paganini was five and a half years old, his father, a commercial broker, began teaching him to play the mandolin (sometimes called mandoline, a type of lute).

His mother and father, each with a different temperament, guided their son steadily toward success. Teresa, unable to read and write, a mere child herself, did everything possible to bring the best to her gifted son. Paganini's father, Antonio, when not at his usual job on the docks, stayed at home. He taught his children to read and write. He also played the mandolin and, an incurable gambler, figured numbers for winning combinations to the lottery. Listening to his son play the violin, hearing sounds more sensitive than those produced by an experienced musician, Antonio realized the enormity of his son's gift. He placed in Paganini's tiny hands his mandolin.

Although Niccolò had nearly died from measles and later would be deathly sick with scarlet fever, one cannot measure the favorable impact of Antonio's act. One also cannot imagine the dedication and adult support required from Antonio once Niccolò began to produce music. Antonio's teaching proved decisive. Learning more rapidly than the music could be taught, the child played all compositions put before him after only a few months' instruction. Soon, he went beyond performing to composing. Before he was eight years old, with his father's guidance, he wrote a sonata. Francesco Bennati wrote in May 1851, thirty years later: "Paganini's progress was so rapid that he would be hard put to say how it all came about. There was an element of spontaneity about it that was beyond comprehension, as though his talent progressed entirely unawares (Kenneson, p. 68).

Antonio taught Niccolò the mandolin for a year and a half. At this time, the child probably learned the instrument's fretted fingerboard and thoroughly mastered the intricate finger plucking that mandolinists must become proficient in to produce quality music. While still seven years old, he received his first violin; after this, using a bow for delicately articulated playing, his learning accelerated even more. He learned to play the new violin and then, because he had no music and could afford no music, he composed his own.

Paganini's unimaginable ability to perform virtuoso feats on the violin surpassed any plateau adults had accomplished even after extensive practice. The child's tenacity at practice and his ability at composing probably left Antonio exhausted. He had provided his son only a few years of improvised teaching, and the results ran beyond any dream he may have had. Even the boy's many childhood teachers, not really knowing what to do with him, cast him about from composing all sorts of pieces to playing the violin.

Because young boys sometimes took jobs in Genoa's theater orchestras, the idea that the young Paganini could work for money probably prompted Antonio to decide to stop teaching his son as early as 1792. At this time he chose Giovanni Cervetto, a somewhat accomplished theater violinist, to give his son lessons.

Cervetto was Paganini's first genuine violin instructor, demonstrating for the boy the proper art of bowing. He also introduced the nearly untutored child to the lyric theater and musical plays, a form of art so fascinating it held Paganini's attention for the rest of his life.

After a short time, feeling inadequate, Cervetto turned the extra-ordinary child over to a younger friend, Francesco Gnecco, a second-ary opera composer. Gnecco, a busy composer, and perhaps understanding he could do little for his extraordinarily gifted pupil, introduced him to Genoa's leading violinist, Giocomo Costa. This man gave Paganini thirty lessons and invited him to play in several churches in Genoa; enjoying the performances, sometimes Paganini played two or three times a week. In 1794, Costa prepared him for a performance of a Joseph Pleyel (1757–1831) Concerto at the Church of St. Filippo Neri.

Paganini's early violin teachers were far less significant than what occurred in 1795, when he was only thirteen years old, after hearing Franco-Polish violinist Auguste Frédéric Durand in Genoa. In 1794, when Durand, a brilliant performer, toured Germany and Italy, his contemporaries, immensely impressed, attempted to analyze and duplicate his expertise and method. Durand's powerful display of strength and perfection also stirred the imagination of young Niccolò. Later, he allegedly told François-Joseph Fétis, a Belgian music theorist and historian, that he had felt some influence from Durand. Indeed, he devised many of his most accomplished and successful effects after hearing this master in concert.

Yet as early as age thirteen, Paganini based his concert repertoire on his own violin compositions because these pieces displayed his brilliant virtuosity to the best advantage. Although he continued for a time to perform concertos by French violinist Jacques Pierre Rode (1774–1830) and violinist Rodolphe Kreutzer (1766–1831), he com-posed movements as additions to them for one purpose: to construct each composition to fit his own personal style.

As Paganini's career flourished, so did the strictness of his father. The youth played his violin from morning until night every day of the week under the stern eye of his father. If Antonio didn't think the child practiced hard and long enough, he compelled him to redouble his efforts by not feeding him. In fact, as a teenager, Paganini withstood severe physical punishment and stress. As one might expect, it wasn't long into a period of practice with starvation as punishment that his health began to fail.

Practicing every day, Paganini gradually removed himself from the classical traditions taught by his Genoese violin teachers. Antonio lo-cated a new teacher, this time a truly distinguished violinist. The concertmaster of the royal orchestra in Parma, Alessandro Rolla, be-came his son's teacher. Antonio would travel with him because it was not safe for a thirteen-year-old boy to travel alone, especially when Napoléon Bonaparte planned moves far beyond France. By 1795 the French planned to open a major front in Italy, and Parma, in the north, became vulnerable to soldiers. By 1797, when Napoleon was given command of the new army of Italy, pedestrian travel became even more precarious. But travel and lodging required money, of which the family had very little. Therefore, to raise funds, Antonio had Paganini practice in order to give a benefit concert at Genoa's Teatro di Sant'Agostino. (He probably also received financial assistance from the generous Marquis Gian Carlo di Negro, a wealthy patron of musicians to whom Paganini had been introduced earlier.)

In 1795, at age thirteen, Paganini gave his benefit concert. Giving this performance, leaving his home, and traveling to Parma formed critical directions in his career. An important notice was printed in Genoa's newspaper, *Avvisi*, on July 25, 1795, advertising Paganini's concert in the Teatro di Sant'Agostino for Friday, July 31. The notice stated that Niccolò Paganini of Genoa, a boy (the article didn't state that he was thirteen), would give a concert. The notice added that he was already famous in his *paese* (native city) for his virtuosity as a violinist.

No information exists regarding this early debut other than the Genoa newspaper notice and Paganini's two personal accounts. Most of his performances in Italy took place as intermezzo concerts (short, light music between the acts of a play or opera). For these concerts, either the singer Teresa Bertinotti or one of the last of the performing castrati, Luigi Marchesi, were with him on stage. Paganini's intermezzo concert possibly featured the Pleyel concerto he had learned from Costa and his own *Carmagnole Variations*, a composition influenced by a contemporary French revolutionary piece.

As the benefit concert was a success and enough money had been raised, Paganini and his father traveled to Parma in September. In the city Paganini met

> ♪
> **Niccolò Paganini**
>
> **Born:**
> October 27, 1782
> Genoa, Italy
> **Died:**
> May 27, 1840
> Nice, France
> **Only Important Work
> Published
> in His Lifetime:**
> *Twenty-Four Caprices*

Alessandro Rolla, the violinist, who was sick in bed. The boy found a violin and the maestro's latest concerto on a table. Niccolò, after approval from his father, picked up Rolla's violin and played the composition by sight. Even though painfully ill, Rolla came alert and was astonished to discover the person sight-reading the concerto was only a child. He told the child he had nothing to teach him, at which time he advised him to visit Italian composer Ferdinando Paër (1771–1839). Paër, born in Parma only eleven years earlier than Paganini and a truly great musician, had already composed forty operas and served at the court of Napoleon I as musical director.

Ferdinando Paër at the time was director of the Parma Conservatory. Interested in the child's ability, he listened to the boy play, spoke to Paganini and his father, and, immensely impressed, immediately referred the child to his own teacher, the Neapolitan conductor Gasparo Ghiretti. For six months, Ghiretti worked with Paganini three times a week. They studied counterpoint (a melody accompanying another melody note for note) in detail. Paganini loved counterpoint and composed—just to pass his time and as an étude, or exercise—twenty-four fugues for four hands, with no instrument, just using ink, pen, and paper. Shortly after this, Paër, hearing of the boy's rapid progress and uncanny ability to compose, insisted Paganini come once every morning and again in the afternoon for intensive lessons in composition.

Niccolò's move to Parma provided no violin teacher, but it brought his musical abilities to the attention of experienced composers. Far from home, still tyrannized by the excessive severity of his father's prodding, Niccolò, fourteen years old, found happiness and gratification in his work as his enormous gift developed and his knowledge of music and composition increased.

After being away from his family in Genoa for nearly a year, Paganini came down with severe pneumonia. His father took him home to Genoa, where he remained for many months. During the long duration of his illness, if he performed at all, it was only at private affairs. The Marquis di Negro possibly arranged private concerts for him in order to provide quality music for personal acquaintances. However, when the French violinist Rodolphe Kreutzer arrived in Genoa on November 27, 1796, during a music festival honoring Josephine Bonaparte, the Marquis di Negro, charged with providing entertainment for Kreutzer, arranged a performance by Paganini.

In June 1799, with Genoa under siege, Napoleon's army threatened nearby Tortona and Novi. National guard soldiers showed no mercy for criminals and rioters. All young men age seventeen and over found themselves in the army. Because of this, and thinking of Niccolò, Antonio decided to move his family to Ramairone in the Polcevera Valley. There, Antonio and his two sons began a new life as farmers.

At Ramairone, Paganini picked up the guitar and in no time became a master. As with the violin, he created his own playing method based on a personal, highly developed fingering technique. In the end, however, Paganini never really liked playing the guitar. Years later, he only played the instrument occasionally and then not to amuse himself or to practice, but to untangle some compositional aspects of the accompaniment of his concertos, especially chordal progressions. However, with the guitar as an exception, he used no instrument for composing. As he composed, he sang or whistled to accompany himself.

As he neared his twentieth birthday, Paganini remained unknown. He had found no personal sponsor and performed as a violinist only in insignificant towns where one could, on short notice, rent a hall and, with a poster or two, hope for a substantial audience. In 1800, when Paganini was eighteen years old, his father left Ramairone to look for work on the docks at Livorno (Leghorn). By this time, the seaport at Genoa had been closed by French soldiers. Not too many days after Antonio left, Niccolò followed him carrying a letter of introduction to the British consul, whom the French had not forced out of the city. Surprisingly, the British consul helped him engage a hall for two summer concert appearances.

After the summer performances, in December, at the Teatro Ran in Modena Goni, Paganini performed twice with singer Andrea Reggiantini assisting him. It was during the second concerts that he played his new *Fandango Spagnolo*, which, improvised and cleanly unaccompanied, featured imitated violin bird songs. The audience could not have been more elated.

By the end of 1800, with enormous success in public appearances, Paganini came to a difficult decision. In order to move forward, he knew he had to leave his father. At age eighteen, the intrepid young violinist left the security of his home and parents to seek freedom and independence. Not once did he hesitate. Six months later (September 1801), he competed in Lucca at the Feast of the Holy Cross at the annual music festival. After realizing the success of this performance, he knew he had left his family and security for good reason. Now, he knew he wanted to become part of an orchestra. He had seen an advertisement for a position in the orchestra of the famed Lucca's Teatro Nazionale. Far too young (he was only eighteen), he was nevertheless overcome with a determination to win the position. Daily practice for the competition pushed him practically beyond his own capacity. But when the time came, he won. To top off the whole affair, at the Feast of the Holy Cross, in a solemn pontifical mass, the theater presented him. Before his appearance, Minister of the Interior Adriano Mencarelli asked the clergy if Paganini would perform following the Kyrie (Kyrie Eleison is a part of the Roman Catholic service).

With the agreement made, after the Kyrie, Paganini played for nearly half an hour and gave an astonishing performance of his own personal musical mimicry. His violin imitated the flute, the trombone, the horn, even a chirping bird. Every person in attendance

> ♪
> **Interesting Facts about Niccolò Paganini**
>
> He almost died from a case of the measles when he was five years old.
>
> He received his first violin at the age of seven; because he had no music and couldn't afford to buy it, he composed his own.
>
> From a very young age, he could sight-read (perform a piece of music without previous preparation or study) the most difficult music written.

enjoyed the unusual and exciting performance, yet some classical diehards called Paganini to question for misusing his instrument. Some called the entertainment a type of spectacle one might find at a circus sideshow. On the other hand, a few enthusiasts thought Paganini should have reserved the extraordinary achievement for the theater. In the end, the Jacobins, a group of extreme political radicals in the audience, saved the day by standing and leading a long and thunderous applause.

The following year, in April 1802, the twenty-year-old musician traveled to Leghorn, where a new theater neared its opening performances. It was on this excursion that he acquired a violin, a fine Guarneri.

"'Once finding myself in Leghorn without a violin a Monsieur Livron lent me an instrument to play a Viotti concerto and then made me a present of it'" (Kenneson, p. 73).

In Lucca, Niccolò loved the family he stayed with, the Quilicis. The bond between them became so strong that they never gave up their devotion to him. For their daughter, Eleanora Quiliei (Alla Ragazza Eleanora), he composed and dedicated Six Sonatas for Violin and Guitar, op. 3. Many at the time believed Eleanora became his first love; and although no proof exists, it must be mentioned that she was the only individual outside his immediate family mentioned in his will.

It wasn't long before good luck came in his direction in the form of an appointment at court. Napoléon Bonaparte changed Lucca to a principality and appointed Princess Elise Baciocchi hereditary ruler. Niccolò composed chamber music while living in Lucca. Especially noteworthy among the works were many sonatas (including the beautiful *Napoleon Sonata*). He also composed quartets for strings and guitar, as well as the still-memorable *Duetto Amoroso* dedicated to Princess Elise. Continuing his work, in 1809 he became a conductor at the Teatro Castiglioncello and took on the job of leading a performance of Cimarosa's opera *Il Matimonio Segreto* (The Secret Marriage).

Evidence of Paganini's musical genius and prowess can be heard in all his musical compositions, but especially in *Twenty-Four Caprices* for unaccompanied violin. Most historians believe he composed *Caprices* before he was twenty years old. These creations, a veritable encyclopedia of violin playing, include complex works that reveal the fundamental transformation in violin technique for which Paganini became known. The works in their original form have made a lasting impression on scholars, musicians, and audiences throughout the world. Indeed, in the nineteenth century, Robert Schumann claimed the theme of the second caprice alone ensured Paganini indefinite status and historical importance on the world stage of music.

Concerning his role as composer, Paganini said his one great rule was perfect unity within diversity, something that even he as a genius considered a difficult achievement. In 1830, Paganini told the world he would not play compositions by other composers and had, in fact, destroyed all music he possessed written by hands other than his own. He retired in 1835 and a short time thereafter lost his voice.

On April 27, 1837, Niccolò Paganini wrote his last will and testament. He left his violin, an instrument made in 1742 by Joseph Guarneri del Gesù, to the city of Genoa, hoping it would be preserved forever. The Guarneri is still in the town hall there.

In 1840, Paganini died at Nice, France, of cancer of the larynx, leaving Europe temporarily without a leading violinist, without a master to conquer the concert stage. When he died, playing his violin in his last hour, he had in his possession twenty-two violins, violas, cellos, and guitars—all priceless instruments by Amati, Guadagnini, Guarneri, Roggeri, Ruggeri, Stradivari, and Tonomi.

After his death, the Catholic Church, for five years unsatisfied concerning his devotion, would not allow his body to be buried in sacred ground. Eventually, his body was interred on his own estate in an ordinary village graveyard.

Bibliography

Fisher, Renee B. *Musical Prodigies: Masters at an Early Age.* New York: Association Press, 1973.

Kenneson, Claude. *Musical Prodigies: Perilous Journeys, Remarkable Lives.* Portland, Oreg.: Amadeus Press, 1998.

Sadie, Stanley, ed. *Grove Concise Dictionary of Music.* London: Macmillan Press, 1983.

Schwarz, Boris. *Great Masters of the Violin.* New York: Simon & Schuster, 1983.

♪

Isaac Stern

(1920–2001)

Although violinist Isaac Stern emigrated from Russia (then the Soviet Union) with his parents as a small child, he took his training and spent his formative years as a musician in the United States. He said, "All my formative years as an artist were spent in America, at a time when there was an ingathering of musical influences from virtually every country in Europe" (Stern, p. 4). Today, many historians consider Stern the first genius of American violinists. Further, they agree that his virtuosity, style, and taste are inimitable.

Stern's infinite energy is legendary. During a long, successful, and extremely productive career, he made over one hundred recordings and performed all over the world for presidents and other important state dignitaries. Tirelessly, he played as many as two hundred concerts in one year.

Stern was born in Kreminiecz (or Kremenets), a small town on the Polish-Russian border, on July 21, 1920. During the years following the Bolshevik Revolution, 1918–1920, political control of Kreminiecz changed hands frequently, about every two weeks. During a two-week period of Polish rule, Stern was born.

His parents, both well-educated Russians, always held music in the highest reverence. His father, Solomon, was born in Kiev. His mother, Clara, was born in Kreminiecz. Both spoke Russian. Neither spoke English. They knew Yiddish but did not speak the language in the home of the young Stern. Isaac's father, a contractor by trade, had a deep interest in music and painting. Isaac's mother studied voice with the Russian composer Aleksandr Glazunov (1865–1936) in St. Petersburg,

Russia, at the Imperial Conservatory. During the week of Isaac's birth, she received a much coveted scholarship to study singing at the Imperial Conservatory. It was during this time, however, that St. Petersburg remained a city closed to Jews. However, Clara finally gained permission and studied at the Conservatory, although only by very special decree.

In the midst of the Russian civil war and shortly after the failed Bolshevik invasion of Poland, Stern's father obtained a Polish passport and a visa to the United States. Stern's parents wanted to leave their country because they had nothing to do with Soviet life or any part of the Communist cause. Moreover, religion played no part in Stern's childhood: His family never observed any of the traditional Jewish rituals or belonged to any synagogue. The child's attention and education were never focused on anything specifically Jewish. It seems that from the day he was born, Isaac Stern was set on being a musician.

Isaac Stern

After months of travel thousands of miles by train through the frozen flats of Siberia and by boat across the Pacific Ocean, the family arrived in San Francisco. Stern was only ten months old. His father, a dilettante artist and a lover of art, knew a little about paint and color, so to earn money he became a housepainter.

Throughout the Depression years, when jobs were scarce, the family suffered hardships, but music always dominated their life. Sometimes Stern's mother sang while his father played the piano. It was thus that Isaac's music lessons began at home.

Fortunately, both Stern's parents considered music essential to their son's childhood education. They taught and encouraged him. Interestingly enough, while taking lessons, Stern did not demonstrate any gift for the piano. And he had no interest in the violin until he was eight years old, when his friend Nathan Koblick played the instrument. Stern says that because Nathan played, he too wanted to play the violin. Stern had Nathan to thank for inspiring him to play the instrument, yet he doesn't remember acquiring his first violin.

> [He says] probably my family got it for me. . . . I had one teacher
> for a while, then another, and another. Those teachers—none of
> them particularly effective—found that I was progressing be-
> yond their capacity to teach me. (Stern, p. 10)

Then Stern's mother and father enrolled him in the Sunday school
of San Francisco's Reform Synagogue, the Temple Emanu-El. A highly
gifted student, he learned to read Hebrew in record time. The cantor
(a singer of liturgical solos in a synagogue) at the temple was a man
who loved music. One day, as Stern played the violin in the temple,
Cantor Rinder heard him and knew he was listening to that special
music of the extremely gifted. He also realized the family could not
afford instruction for the boy. Wanting to help, he explained the situation to a wealthy lady, a patron of the arts.

When Stern played for her, she immediately offered to be responsible for him, both financially and personally. The woman, Lutie D.
Goldstein, brought Stern to the attention of the San Francisco Conservatory of Music. After this, she supported him for many years in his
musical studies.

Music was always part of Stern's life. His parents scraped together
money to go to concerts. They played the works of Stokowski and
Toscanini at home on a crank-up Victrola. And when his mother and
father discovered Stern's exceptional talent, they took interest in his
growth, encouraged him, and monitored his hours of practice.

When ten years old, while practicing, Stern accidentally discovered
he could play the violin in a way no one had taught him.

> One day when I was ten years old, I suddenly discovered that
> I could do things on my own with the violin, things no one had
> taught me—move the bow in certain new ways; feel my fin-
> gers on the strings; bring forth shades of sound. . . . Suddenly
> one day I became my own master. I wanted to play; I wanted
> to learn how to play better. I wanted to do it because I was be-
> ginning to revel in my own abilities. (Stern, p. 13)

Experimenting with his new technique using bow and fingers, he
moved forward on his own into notes and subtleties no one imagined
possible on the violin. At the same time, he wanted to play the instrument with technical exactness. Sensing the potential of what he might
be able to accomplish if he practiced and experimented enough, he
started practicing on his own.

For the purpose of practicing, Stern had been withdrawn from
school at the age of eight. His mother and father felt his time would
be better spent working with his violin. When the San Francisco

Board of Education decided to test him at age ten with the Stanford-Binet intelligence test, he showed the intellectual capacity of a sixteen-year-old. Thus the school board decided he could continue with his home studies.

A few months later, Stern gave his debut recital. For this occasion the *San Francisco Chronicle* sent a music critic to the event. The critic's review the following day praised Stern as "'a boy violinist of exceptional talent' [with] excellent technical control of the instrument" (Stern, p. 13).

It was at this time that Stern went to hear the pianist Ruth Slenczynska. Her father, hearing that Stern was a violinist, looked at his hands and told him he'd never be a fiddle player. Stern writes:

> a picture of me, taken one year later, when I was eleven . . . appeared in the San Francisco *Call-Bulletin* [with the] statement that "Isaac Stern, talented 11 year old violinist . . . will give a recital at the Community Playhouse next Thursday night." . . . The music critic of the *Chronicle*, Alexander Fried, wrote that the violin recital "proved that he belongs to the higher order of precocious talents." (Stern, p. 14)

Stern entered the San Francisco Conservatory of Music at age ten to study with the Russian violinist Naoum Blinder, who had been a pupil at the Moscow Conservatory. Stern's training with Blinder remained in the early twentieth-century tradition of the Moscow-Odessa school of violin. From 1932 until 1937, Stern worked exclusively with Blinder (with only a brief interlude with Louis Persinger, Yehudi Menuhin's teacher), and after the later 1930s he had no further formal training. He said that while at the Conservatory, something nearly beyond his control seemed to happen under his fingers.

His progress, rather than leaping forth, was slow but tenacious and steady. Blinder's teaching methods neglected exercises, études, or little studies for practice and scales. Instead, he focused on cultivating Stern's independence, his natural technique, and his musical instinct. Blinder only stopped him if he began going in the wrong direction. He taught Stern to teach himself; and this, Stern believed, was the most important gift a teacher could give a student.

Although his formal training ended, Stern's education did not. He learned in concert halls in front of an audience. He learned behind the music stand. He listened to the Budapest Quartet performing the complete cycle of Beethoven quartets and to Rachmaninoff playing Beethoven's piano sonatas. He attended recitals by Artur Schnabel, Bronislaw Huberman, and Fritz Kreisler; and he heard Richard Wagner's (1813–1883) *Der Ring des Nibelungen* (1853–1874) performed by Lotte Lehmann, Lauritz Melchoir, and Korsten Flagstad at the San Francisco Opera.

At the same time, Stern's childhood remained calm, without the stress of imperative success. Blinder helped create for the young Stern during his formative years a peaceful environment of fraternity with the musicians of the orchestra. Stern frequently played chamber music with these musicians, and they treated him as an equal even though he was two generations younger than any of them. In their company he learned the chamber music repertoire, attended orchestra and opera rehearsals, and heard and met the important soloists of the day.

In March 1937, Stern, seventeen years old, played his first professional concert with the San Francisco Symphony Orchestra under Pierre Monteux. The concert, one of a series, was broadcast live coast to coast, sponsored by the Junior Chamber of Commerce of San Francisco. What America heard was a teenage boy playing the Brahms Violin Concerto.

By the time he was seventeen, Stern had appeared in different places in and around San Francisco and people were beginning to acknowledge his talent. Most agreed he should go to New York and make his debut there. Lutie Goldstein gave him a Giovanni Baptista Guadagnina violin for which she had paid $6,500. Thereafter, Stern and his mother went to New York, where he played at Town Hall with a seating capacity of fifteen hundred. The reviewers said he should go back to San Francisco and practice. Indeed, some of New York's most eminent critics said he had crossed the "Great Divide" into the lofty realm of the artist, adding that his playing was erratic. Yet Stern decided to keep trying and give the career another year or two. He went back to San Francisco.

> ♪
> **Isaac Stern**
>
> **Born:**
> July 21, 1920
> Kreminiecz, Russia
>
> **Died:**
> September 22, 2001
> New York City
>
> **Number of Recordings:**
> Over 100

Stern said that from his earliest years he had been able to speak to music without being told how, that music had always been easy for him. He learned at this time that longer, more concentrated hours of practice didn't matter. The important aspect for him was concentration. He discovered that his main weakness was a lack of concentration.

On January 8, 1943, Stern made a triumphant debut at Carnegie Hall in New York City. He selected works that would serve as reaffirmation of the reason he was a musician, works that would prove to himself and to others that he had a right to be there. Alexander Zakin accompanied him on the piano. One year later, Stern played again at Carnegie Hall, and at that performance critics called him one of the world's master fiddle players. This concert, at the age of twenty-four, catapulted him into major recognition.

Stern played only seven concerts the first year, fourteen the next. In between he practiced day and night. After his wartime performances for Allied troops in Greenland, Iceland, and the South Pacific, Stern was deluged by tour and recording offers. He made his screen debut in the 1946 film *Humoresque*, in which his hands were photographed as those of John Garfield, who portrayed an ambitious young violinist involved with a wealthy patroness, played by Joan Crawford.

By 1947, Stern was playing ninety concerts a year. He made his European debut in 1948 at the Lucerne, Switzerland Festival, under Charles Munch, and went on to perform in nine European countries that summer. His 1949 concert tour comprised 120 concerts in seven months throughout the United States, Europe, and South America. When Stern had his twenty-fifth birthday, he was recognized as one of the great violinists of his generation.

By the 1970s, Stern was said to be the world's highest-paid violinist, earning as much as ten thousand dollars a performance and playing as many as two hundred concerts a year. Between concerts he still practiced long and hard. He worked best under pressure, practicing anywhere from half an hour to fourteen hours a day, preferring to do so at night and in the early hours of the morning. His two most prized instruments were his Giuseppe del Gesù violins.

Stern loved violin music of all periods. He seemed to perceive all music with an instinctual sense of perfect tone, gesture, and expression. He understood his gift and cared for it well. Flexibility and full command of his instrument were always Stern's main objective. Completely adaptable and well trained, he had been known to work out perfect new fingerings of difficult passages spontaneously during performances.

Stern's 1968 silver anniversary concert at Carnegie Hall, commemorating his first appearance there twenty-five years earlier, was a landmark of his career. For that concert, he and Alexander Zakin revived the violin arrangement of Brahms's op. 120, no. 2, for clarinet and piano. They also presented Bach's Sonata in E, along with Hungarian composer Béla Bartók's Second Sonata, two Mozart movements, and French composer Maurice Ravel's (1875–1937) *Tzigant*. The ease and perfection with which Stern changed styles created an impressive, memorable recital.

Stern had a down-to-earth stage presence. He walked matter-of-factly on and off stage, his violin held in front of him like a staff in his left hand, his right hand grasping the bow. During performance, he planted his feet wide apart, stood sturdy as an oak tree, and began his sublime music without any showy theatrics.

Although star soloists are reputed to have huge egos, incompatible with the close cooperation performing requires, Stern never experienced such a problem. He has said he feels that each kind of music has its own dynamics, its own form, its own joys. Being able to perform as a soloist, and knowing the power one has as a soloist, makes the musical experience that much grander.

During the 1960s, Stern enriched his already perfect performance repertoire by forming a trio with the pianist Eugene Istomin and the cellist Leonard Rose. Initiated at the Israel Festival in 1961, the trio played together until 1983. The trio achieved particular acclaim for the Beethoven programs it performed around the world in 1970 and 1971 in honor of the 200th anniversary of the composer's birth.

In the 1970s and 1980s, Stern began playing shows on television, particularly series such as *Tonight at Carnegie Hall* and *Live from Lincoln Center*. Besides television, he worked in movies. The motion picture *From Mao to Mozart: Isaac Stern in China* chronicles the violinist's 1979 tour of the People's Republic of China, during which time he gave master classes to young Chinese musicians. The film won an Academy Award for best full-length documentary of 1981 and won special mention at Cannes. Years later, Stern was the subject of a second documentary in 1991 with the release of *Isaac Stern: A Life*.

Stern has also used his violin as an effective cultural and political tool. In 1956, before the establishment of official cultural exchanges, he performed in the Soviet Union. Stern also became a mentor to several upcoming young musicians. Among his protégés is the violinist Pinchas Zukerman, discovered as a child prodigy in Israel.

Determined to safeguard Carnegie Hall from threatened demolition in 1960, Stern organized the Citizens' Committee to Save Carnegie Hall. When he succeeded and became president of the Carnegie Hall corporation, detractors accused him of having a conflict of interests. Critics said he filled the hall's schedule with concerts by himself and his friends, including events like Isaac Stern and His Friends, a chamber music series designed to evoke the informality of a living-room gathering. Defenders insisted that Stern had nothing to do with programming decisions. Everyone agreed he was too honest for that. Later, Stern cut back his personal involvement. He did, however, pioneer a multi-million-dollar project in the late 1980s to repair the structure and protect the hall from ruinous vibrations of the subways below.

> ♪
> **Interesting Facts about Isaac Stern**
>
> He showed no real musical interest or talent at a very young age despite taking piano lessons; he only became interested in the violin at the age of eight because he had a friend who played it.
>
> He was withdrawn from school at the age of eight so he could practice the violin, and he never attended high school or college.
>
> He helped save Carnegie Hall in New York City from threatened demolition.

Stern campaigned for a number of Democratic presidential candidates, including Lyndon B. Johnson and Hubert Humphrey. He also put his causes on presidential agendas. Having introduced the idea of an arts council during John F. Kennedy's presidency, Stern founded and oversaw the creation of the National Council on the Arts. This organization became the precursor of the National Endowment for the Arts, created during the Johnson administration. Stern's support of the arts extended to testifying before Congress in February 1970. At this time, he urged the legislature to raise its allocation of federal funds to the arts, warning that the United States stood poised to become an industrial complex without a soul.

Israel also has been the object of Stern's passion, to the point that he was a one-man diplomatic service to the Jewish state. In addition to performing there frequently, he was the chairman, since 1964, of the America-Israel Cultural Foundation, which raises funds for Israeli cultural organizations and subsidizes Israeli musicians. In 1973, he founded the Jerusalem Music Center, where musicians from several nations taught master classes.

In 1996, the San Francisco Conservatory of Music established the Isaac Stern Distinguished Chair in Violin to fund a professorship in violin in honor of Stern. In April 1999, Stern traveled to Germany for the first time. He visited the houses of Mendelssohn, Beethoven, and Brahms to see their harpsichords and pianos.

Stern regretted that he never had basic training in violin playing. However, that lack gave him the freedom to experience the musical insights that constituted his strength and pleasure. Isaac Stern died of heart failure at New York Weill Cornell Medical Center on September 22, 2001.

Bibliography

Kenneson, Claude. *Musical Prodigies: Perilous Journeys, Remarkable Lives.* Portland, Oreg.: Amadeus Press, 1998.

Schwarz, Boris. *Great Masters of the Violin.* New York: Simon & Schuster, 1983.

Stern, Isaac, and Chaim Potok. *Isaac Stern, My First 79 Years.* New York: Alfred A. Knopf, 1999.

♪

Glossary

Absolute Pitch, Sense of. The faculty some people possess of being able to sing any note asked for, or of being able to recognize any note heard. It is actually a form of memory; the possessor of absolute pitch retains in his or her mind (consciously or unconsciously) the pitch of an instrument, (e.g., the piano) and relates to that instrument every sound in music he or she hears. At age seven, Mozart awed everyone who knew him with his sense of absolute pitch.

Air. The main melody of a harmonized composition in the sense of a tuneful, flowing, usually soprano or treble part of a composition; or a composition itself of a melodious character.

Autoharp. A type of zither (a wooden box with strings). The instrument has no special melody strings. One picks out the melody notes by applying more force. Chords are played by depressing keys that damp all the strings except those in use.

Bass. Can be spelled *base*. German is *bass*, French is *basse*, Italian is *basso*. Bass is the lowest part of the harmony, whether vocal or instrumental. Bass is the most important and the foundation of what lies above it, as chords are reckoned from their bass note. The harmonics set up by this lowest note are prominent and exercise a predominant influence on the flavor of the chord as a whole.

Cadenza. An improvised musical flourish, generally near the end of a composition. Short cadenzas were elaborate, but short, musical flourishes in improvised style that Bach, for instance, played near the end of a composition. These gave him the chance to demonstrate his technical brilliance as an organist.

Cantata. A choral work based on a narrative text that is dramatic, religious, or humorous. The cantata is composed of arias, choruses, solos, duets, and recitatives as well as other movements.

Cembalo. Italian for *harpsichord*.

Chromatic Progressions. A way to move harmoniously from chord to chord, or melodic tone to melodic tone, through the use of sharps, or semitones found on the chromatic scale.

Clavichord. The earliest type of stringed keyboard instrument; a forerunner of the piano, probably developed in the twelfth century. The tone of a clavichord is very soft. Unlike the harpsichord, limited gradations of loud and soft can be produced by changing the pressure on the keys.

Clavier. In Bach's time, *clavier* was a synonym for *clavichord* or *harpsichord*. It also meant keyboard. Therefore, compositions for the clavier could be played on harpsichord, clavichord, or organ—all keyboard instruments.

Counterpoint. The art of combining many melodic lines into one harmonious whole. Counterpoint is the art of plural melody.

Détaché. "Detached"; more or less staccato (in the playing of the violin, etc.). Grand *détaché* means with the full bow for every note; *petit détaché*, with the point of the bow for every note; and *détaché sec* is the same as *martelé*, or "hammered." The term refers to a series of short, sharp blows with the bow upon the strings. Musicians use the point of the bow for this process unless the heel is indicated by the expression *martelé au talon*.

Encore. A French word meaning again. In English, *encore* is used to request the repetition of a performance. It may be used to ask the performer to return to the stage to play an additional composition.

Fortepiano. An older name for *pianoforte*, later shortened to *piano*.

Fugue. A composition in which a theme is taken up and developed by the various instruments or voices in succession according to the strict laws of counterpoint.

Harpsichord. A keyboard instrument used in the sixteenth to eighteenth centuries. The harpsichord does not produce increased volume of sound, no matter how hard the keys are struck. In the late eighteenth century, the pianoforte, capable of loud and soft variation, began to take the place of the harpsichord.

Impresario. The organizer, manager, or director of an opera or ballet company or concert series; one who puts on or sponsors an entertainment (e.g., a concert, television show, art exhibition, or sports contest); a producer, director, administrator, maestro, choirmaster, concertmaster, or *coryphaeus* (leader of a chorus in Greek drama).

Improvisation. The art of composing extemporaneously. Some composers added improvised details to already written compositions while playing the organ.

Intermezzo. A short, light dramatic, musical (or ballet) entertainment between the acts of a play or opera. Also, a short movement connecting the main parts of a composition.

Intonation. The manner of producing or uttering tones with regard to rise and fall in pitch; the manner of applying final pitch to a spoken sentence or phrase; a pitch pattern, speech pattern, manner of speaking, tone quality, coloring, melody, or resonance.

Kapellmeister. Also *capellmeister*, or the French *maître de chapelle*. The whole staff of priests, musicians, and other functionaries of a chapel (in Latin *cappa*, or diminutive *capella*) to be called the "King's Chapel," the "Pope's Chapel." Later the term came to be, in common usage, restricted to the musicians; the German term *Kapellmeister* was applied to the musical director. From this, any musical director (even in a theater) came to be called kapellmeister.

Leitmotiv. French, *motif conducteur*; Italian, *motivaguida* or *tema fondamentale*. German for "leading motif," the term refers to a theme, subject, idea, or melody that runs like a thread through a composition.

Libretto. The words of an opera, oratorio, or other long choral work; also, a book containing these words.

Mazurka. One of the traditional national dances of Poland, originally sung as well as danced. It is usually in three-quarter or three-eights time.

Metronome. A clockwork device with an inverted pendulum used to beat time at a rate determined by the position of a sliding weight on the pendulum. The device helps a person maintain regular tempo in practicing on the piano. (In 1945, the Swiss introduced a pocket metronome in the shape of a watch.)

Modulation. The act of changing a key within a composition. Some musicians employ sudden modulations or key changes without a break. Some seventeenth-century compositions have sudden modulations.

Motet. A generally unaccompanied counterpoint song of a sacred nature written with a combination of individual but harmonizing melodies.

Opera Buffa (Italian; *opéra bouffe*, French). Italian and French terms for Comic Opera in the English sense of the words; not the French *opéra-comique*, as distinguished from serious opera.

Opéra Comique. French term that does not mean "comic opera." This opera may be tragic, as for example in Bizet's *Carmen*. This is opera in which the spoken voice is used.

Oratorio. A religious libretto, often based on a biblical theme, set to music. An oratorio is performed in a church without scenery, costumes, or action. Baroque oratorios were more elaborate, both musically and narratively, than, for example, religious cantatas.

Panharmonicon. A mechanical orchestra invented by Johann Nepomuk Mälzel for which Ludwig van Beethoven wrote his *Battle of Vittoria* in 1813. The panharmonicon included flutes, clarinets, trumpets, violins, violoncellos, drums, cymbals, triangle, and strings struck by hammers.

Passion Music. The story of the last days and the death of Jesus Christ, set to music. The libretto is based on the Gospel as told by Sts. Matthew, Mark, Luke, or John. Passion music is traditionally performed on Good Friday.

Pitch. The key used for a song, an instrument, or the voice.

Plainsong. The word is used to indicate the large body of traditional ritual melody of the Western Christian Church. It is a translation of *cantus planus*, in contradistinction to *cantus figuratus* (florid song, implying a counterpoint added to the traditional melody) or *cantus mensuratus* (measured song, implying the regularity of rhythm associated with harmonic music). The term *plain* may be taken in the literal sense of "unadorned."

Prelude. Any piece of music played as a preliminary to any other piece or before any play or ceremony. Since the nineteenth century, a short, romantic composition.

Quodlibet. Comes from the Latin meaning "what you please." A quodlibet is an improvised song with humorous lyrics that sometimes hold double meanings.

Rubato. A technique in music consisting of intentionally and temporarily modifying the length of notes when stating a melody, attacking a note later than expected, or making one note longer and the other shorter and temporarily deviating from a strict tempo.

Scherzo. Italian for "joke." A lively, playful movement in three-quarter time usually following a slow one and sometimes constituting the third section of a sonata, symphony, or quartet. Beethoven is the father of the scherzo.

Scordatura. Literally, "out of tuning." Abnormal tuning of a stringed instrument for the purpose of producing an unusual note, facilitating some type of passage, or changing the general tonal effect.

Syncopated. In music, beginning a tone on an accented beat and continuing it through the next accented beat; also, beginning a tone on the last half of a beat and continuing it through the first half of the following beat.

Tempo. The rate of speed at which a musical composition is played. Tempo may be indicated by such notations on music as *allegro* (fast, brisk, sprightly), and *andante* (moderately slow), or by reference to metronome (a device used to maintain an even tempo) timing.

Timbre (timbral). Tone quality, coarse or smooth, ringing or more subtle, "scarlet" like that of a trumpet, "rich brown" like that of a cello, or "silver" like that of the flute. These color analogies come naturally to every mind. German for "timbre" is *Klangfarbe*; literally, "sound color."

Transpose. To write or play music in a different key.

Tremolo. A tremulous effect produced by the rapid playing of the same tone, as by the rapid up-and-down movement of the bow or plectrum (used for plucking the strings of a guitar, mandolin, etc.).

Variations. An elaborate musical technique whereby a theme can be changed by ornamentation, counterpoint, or the addition of a new melody. In some compositions, such as Bach's *Goldberg Variations*, each variation can stand as an independent composition.

Vibrato (See also tremolo). A tremulous effect obtained by rapidly alternating the original tone with a slightly perceptible variation in the pitch, as in the rapid pulsation of the finger on the string of a violin.

Viol, Viola. Stringed instruments of the sixteenth and seventeenth centuries. Violins replaced viols, as the piano replaced the harpsichord. A viola in current use is part of today's violin family. This instrument is slightly larger than the violin and has a lower range.

Viola da Gamba. A bass viol used in the seventeenth century. It was held on or between the knees when played.

Zither. Also written as *cither* or *cythringen*. This instrument has the flat body of a guitar, the oval shape of a lute, and wire strings that are plucked or strummed.

Index

About the Author

IRENE EARLS received her Ph.D. in the History of Art from the University of Georgia. A professor at the University of Florida, she teaches advanced placement courses to academically gifted high school students. She is the author of *Renaissance Art: A Topical Dictionary* (Greenwood, 1987), *Baroque Art: A Topical Dictionary* (Greenwood, 1996), and *Napoléon III L'Architecte et L'Urbaniste de Paris*.